# MznLnx

*Missing Links Exam Preps*

Exam Prep for

# Operations Management: An Integrated Approach

Reid & Sanders, 3rd Edition

The MznLnx Exam Prep is your link from the texbook and lecture to your exams.
The MznLnx Exam Preps are unauthorized and comprehensive reviews of your textbooks.

All material provided by MznLnx and Rico Publications (c) 2010
Textbook publishers and textbook authors do not particpate in or contribute to these reviews.

# MznLnx

## Rico Publications

*Exam Prep for Operations Management: An Integrated Approach*
3rd Edition
Reid & Sanders

*Publisher:* Raymond Houge
*Assistant Editor:* Michael Rouger
*Text and Cover Designer:* Lisa Buckner
*Marketing Manager:* Sara Swagger
*Project Manager, Editorial Production:* Jerry Emerson
*Art Director:* Vernon Lowerui

*Product Manager:* Dave Mason
*Editorial Asitant:* Rachel Guzmanji
*Pedagogy:* Debra Long
*Cover Image:* Jim Reed/Getty Images
*Text and Cover Printer:* City Printing, Inc.
*Compositor:* Media Mix, Inc.

(c) 2010 Rico Publications

ALL RIGHTS RESERVED. No part of this work covered by the copyright may be reproduced or used in any form or by an means--graphic, electronic, or mechanical, including photocopying, recording, taping, Web distribution, information storage, and retrieval systems, or in any other manner--without the written permission of the publisher.

For more information about our products, contact us at:
Dave.Mason@RicoPublications.com

For permission to use material from this text or product, submit a request online to:
Dave.Mason@RicoPublications.com

Printed in the United States
ISBN:

# Contents

**CHAPTER 1**
*INTRODUCTION TO OPERATIONS MANAGEMENT* — 1

**CHAPTER 2**
*OPERATIONS STRATEGY AND COMPETITIVENESS* — 14

**CHAPTER 3**
*PRODUCT DESIGN AND PROCESS SELECTION* — 21

**CHAPTER 4**
*SUPPLY CHAIN MANAGEMENT* — 33

**CHAPTER 5**
*TOTAL QUALITY MANAGEMENT* — 45

**CHAPTER 6**
*STATISTICAL QUALITY CONTROL* — 55

**CHAPTER 7**
*JUST-IN-TIME AND LEAN SYSTEMS* — 64

**CHAPTER 8**
*FORECASTING* — 72

**CHAPTER 9**
*CAPACITY PLANNING AND FACILITY LOCATION* — 80

**CHAPTER 10**
*FACILITY LAYOUT* — 87

**CHAPTER 11**
*WORK SYSTEM DESIGN* — 90

**CHAPTER 12**
*INDEPENDENT DEMAND INVENTORY MANAGEMENT* — 99

**CHAPTER 13**
*AGGREGATE PLANNING* — 109

**CHAPTER 14**
*RESOURCE PLANNING* — 116

**CHAPTER 15**
*SCHEDULING* — 122

**CHAPTER 16**
*PROJECT MANAGEMENT* — 127

**ANSWER KEY** — 132

# TO THE STUDENT

## COMPREHENSIVE

The *MznLnx* Exam Prep series is designed to help you pass your exams. Editors at MznLnx review your textbooks and then prepare these practice exams to help you master the textbook material. Unlike study guides, workbooks, and practice tests provided by the texbook publisher and textbook authors, *MznLnx* gives you **all** of the material in each chapter in exam form, not just samples, so you can be sure to nail your exam.

## MECHANICAL

The MznLnx Exam Prep series creates exams that will help you learn the subject matter as well as test you on your understanding. Each question is designed to help you master the concept. Just working through the exams, you gain an understanding of the subject--its a simple mechanical process that produces success.

## INTEGRATED STUDY GUIDE AND REVIEW

MznLnx is not just a set of exams designed to test you, its also a comprehensive review of the subject content. Each exam question is also a review of the concept, making sure that you will get the answer correct without having to go to other sources of material. You learn as you go! Its the easiest way to pass an exam.

## HUMOR

Studying can be tedious and dry. MznLnx's instructional design includes moderate humor within the exam questions on occassion, to break the tedium and revitalize the brain

## Chapter 1. INTRODUCTION TO OPERATIONS MANAGEMENT

1. _____ is an area of business concerned with the production of goods and services, and involves the responsibility of ensuring that business operations are efficient in terms of using as little resource as needed, and effective in terms of meeting customer requirements. It is concerned with managing the process that converts inputs (in the forms of materials, labour and energy) into outputs (in the form of goods and services.)

Operations traditionally refers to the production of goods and services separately, although the distinction between these two main types of operations is increasingly difficult to make as manufacturers tend to merge product and service offerings.

   a. A Stake in the Outcome
   b. A4e
   c. AAAI
   d. Operations management

2. An _____, or organogram(me)) is a diagram that shows the structure of an organization and the relationships and relative ranks of its parts and positions/jobs. The term is also used for similar diagrams, for example ones showing the different elements of a field of knowledge or a group of languages. The French Encyclopédie had one of the first _____s of knowledge in general.
   a. AAAI
   b. A4e
   c. A Stake in the Outcome
   d. Organizational chart

3. A _____ is a list of the general tasks and responsibilities of a position. Typically, it also includes to whom the position reports, specifications such as the qualifications needed by the person in the job, salary range for the position, etc. A _____ is usually developed by conducting a job analysis, which includes examining the tasks and sequences of tasks necessary to perform the job.
   a. Recruitment
   b. Recruitment advertising
   c. Job description
   d. Recruitment Process Insourcing

4. _____, commonly known as e-commerce, consists of the buying and selling of products or services over electronic systems such as the Internet and other computer networks. The amount of trade conducted electronically has grown extraordinarily with widespread Internet usage. The use of commerce is conducted in this way, spurring and drawing on innovations in electronic funds transfer, supply chain management, Internet marketing, online transaction processing, electronic data interchange (EDI), inventory management systems, and automated data collection systems.

## Chapter 1. INTRODUCTION TO OPERATIONS MANAGEMENT

a. A Stake in the Outcome
b. Online shopping
c. A4e
d. Electronic Commerce

5. A _____ is the system of organizations, people, technology, activities, information and resources involved in moving a product or service from supplier to customer. _____ activities transform natural resources, raw materials and components into a finished product that is delivered to the end customer. In sophisticated _____ systems, used products may re-enter the _____ at any point where residual value is recyclable.

a. Wholesalers
b. Supply chain
c. Packaging
d. Drop shipping

6. _____ is an advertisement in which a particular product specifically mentions a competitor by name for the express purpose of showing why the competitor is inferior to the product naming it.

This should not be confused with parody advertisements, where a fictional product is being advertised for the purpose of poking fun at the particular advertisement, nor should it be confused with the use of a coined brand name for the purpose of comparing the product without actually naming an actual competitor. ('Wikipedia tastes better and is less filling than the Encyclopedia Galactica.')

In the 1980s, during what has been referred to as the cola wars, soft-drink manufacturer Pepsi ran a series of advertisements where people, caught on hidden camera, in a blind taste test, chose Pepsi over rival Coca-Cola.

a. 33 Strategies of War
b. 28-hour day
c. 1990 Clean Air Act
d. Comparative advertising

7. _____ refers to the difference between the cost of materials purchased by a company plus the cost of the labor to assemble a product and the price at which the company sells the product. An example is the price of gasoline at the pump over the price of the oil in it. In national accounts used in macroeconomics, it refers to the contribution of the factors of production, i.e., land, labor, and capital goods, to raising the value of a product and corresponds to the incomes received by the owners of these factors.

## Chapter 1. INTRODUCTION TO OPERATIONS MANAGEMENT

a. Deregulation
b. Minimum wage
c. Rehn-Meidner Model
d. Value added


8. _____ can be regarded as an outcome of mental processes (cognitive process) leading to the selection of a course of action among several alternatives. Every _____ process produces a final choice. The output can be an action or an opinion of choice.
   a. 28-hour day
   b. 33 Strategies of War
   c. 1990 Clean Air Act
   d. Decision making


9. _____ is a contract between two parties, one being the employer and the other being the employee. An employee may be defined as: 'A person in the service of another under any contract of hire, express or implied, oral or written, where the employer has the power or right to control and direct the employee in the material details of how the work is to be performed.' Black's Law Dictionary page 471 (5th ed. 1979.)
   a. Exit interview
   b. Employment counsellor
   c. Employment rate
   d. Employment


10. The _____ was a period in the late 18th and early 19th centuries when major changes in agriculture, manufacturing, mining, and transportation had a profound effect on the socioeconomic and cultural conditions in Britain. The changes subsequently spread throughout Europe, North America, and eventually the world. The onset of the _____ marked a major turning point in human society; almost every aspect of daily life was eventually influenced in some way.
    a. Industrial Revolution
    b. Abraham Harold Maslow
    c. Affiliation
    d. Adam Smith


11. _____ are parts that are for practical purposes identical. They are made to specifications that ensure that they are so nearly identical that they will fit into any device of the same type. One such part can freely replace another, without any custom fitting (such as filing.)

4    Chapter 1. INTRODUCTION TO OPERATIONS MANAGEMENT

   a. A4e
   b. AAAI
   c. Interchangeable parts
   d. A Stake in the Outcome


12. _____ is a theory of management that analyzes and synthesizes workflows, with the objective of improving labour productivity. The core ideas of the theory were developed by Frederick Winslow Taylor in the 1880s and 1890s, and were first published in his monographs, Shop Management and The Principles of _____ Taylor believed that decisions based upon tradition and rules of thumb should be replaced by precise procedures developed after careful study of an individual at work.
   a. Scientific management
   b. Master production schedule
   c. Value engineering
   d. Capacity planning


13. _____ was a Scottish moral philosopher and a pioneer of political economy. One of the key figures of the Scottish Enlightenment, Smith is the author of The Theory of Moral Sentiments and An Inquiry into the Nature and Causes of the Wealth of Nations. The latter, usually abbreviated as The Wealth of Nations, is considered his magnum opus and the first modern work of economics.
   a. Affirmative action
   b. Affiliation
   c. Abraham Harold Maslow
   d. Adam Smith


14. _____, widely known as F. W. Taylor, was an American mechanical engineer who sought to improve industrial efficiency. He is regarded as the father of scientific management, and was one of the first management consultants.

Taylor was one of the intellectual leaders of the Efficiency Movement and his ideas, broadly conceived, were highly influential in the Progressive Era.

   a. Geoffrey Colvin
   b. Frederick Winslow Taylor
   c. Douglas N. Daft
   d. Jonah Jacob Goldberg


15. The _____ is a form of reactivity whereby subjects improve an aspect of their behavior being experimentally measured simply in response to the fact that they are being studied, not in response to any particular experimental manipulation.

*Chapter 1. INTRODUCTION TO OPERATIONS MANAGEMENT*

The term was coined in 1955 by Henry A. Landsberger when analyzing older experiments from 1924-1932 at the Hawthorne Works (outside Chicago.) Hawthorne Works had commissioned a study to see if its workers would become more productive in higher or lower levels of light.

   a. 28-hour day
   b. 33 Strategies of War
   c. 1990 Clean Air Act
   d. Hawthorne effect


16. _____ Movement refers to those researchers of organizational development who study the behavior of people in groups, in particular workplace groups. It originated in the 1920s' Hawthorne studies, which examined the effects of social relations, motivation and employee satisfaction on factory productivity. The movement viewed workers in terms of their psychology and fit with companies, rather than as interchangeable parts.
   a. Hersey-Blanchard situational theory
   b. Work design
   c. Participatory management
   d. Human relations


17. _____ refers to those researchers of organizational development who study the behavior of people in groups, in particular workplace groups. It originated in the 1920s' Hawthorne studies, which examined the effects of social relations, motivation and employee satisfaction on factory productivity. The movement viewed workers in terms of their psychology and fit with companies, rather than as interchangeable parts.
   a. Human relations movement
   b. Path-goal theory
   c. Job satisfaction
   d. Job analysis


18. _____ means increasing the scope of a job through extending the range of its job duties and responsibilities. This contradicts the principles of specialisation and the division of labour whereby work is divided into small units, each of which is performed repetitively by an individual worker. Some motivational theories suggest that the boredom and alienation caused by the division of labour can actually cause efficiency to fall.
   a. Delayering
   b. Mock interview
   c. Centralization
   d. Job enlargement

# Chapter 1. INTRODUCTION TO OPERATIONS MANAGEMENT

19. _____ is an attempt to motivate employees by giving them the opportunity to use the range of their abilities. It is an idea that was developed by the American psychologist Frederick Herzberg in the 1950s. It can be contrasted to job enlargement which simply increases the number of tasks without changing the challenge.

   a. Job enrichment
   b. Cash cow
   c. Catfish effect
   d. C-A-K-E

20. _____, is the discipline of using scientific research-based principles, strategies, and other analytical methods, such as mathematical modeling to improve any organization's ability to enact rational, meaningful business management decisions.

   a. Workflow
   b. Management science
   c. Cross ownership
   d. Trustee

21. _____ is the production of large amounts of standardized products, including and especially on assembly lines. The concepts of _____ are applied to various kinds of products, from fluids and particulates handled in bulk to discrete solid parts to assemblies of such parts

   _____ of assemblies typically uses electric-motor-powered moving tracks or conveyor belts to move partially complete products to workers, who perform simple repetitive tasks.

   a. 28-hour day
   b. 1990 Clean Air Act
   c. 33 Strategies of War
   d. Mass production

22. An _____ is a manufacturing process in which parts (usually interchangeable parts) are added to a product in a sequential manner using optimally planned logistics to create a finished product much faster than with handcrafting-type methods. The _____ developed by Ford Motor Company between 1908 and 1915 made _____s famous in the following decade through the social ramifications of mass production, such as the affordability of the Ford Model T and the introduction of high wages for Ford workers. However, the various preconditions for the development at Ford stretched far back into the 19th century, from the gradual realization of the dream of interchangeability, to the concept of reinventing workflow and job descriptions using analytical methods.

## Chapter 1. INTRODUCTION TO OPERATIONS MANAGEMENT

a. Assembly line
b. A Stake in the Outcome
c. AAAI
d. A4e

23. In economics and sociology, an _____ is any factor (financial or non-financial) that enables or motivates a particular course of action, or counts as a reason for preferring one choice to the alternatives. It is an expectation that encourages people to behave in a certain way. Since human beings are purposeful creatures, the study of _____ structures is central to the study of all economic activity (both in terms of individual decision-making and in terms of co-operation and competition within a larger institutional structure.)

a. AAAI
b. A Stake in the Outcome
c. Incentive
d. A4e

24. _____ is a business management strategy aimed at embedding awareness of quality in all organizational processes. _____ has been widely used in manufacturing, education, hospitals, call centers, government, and service industries, as well as NASA space and science programs.

As defined by the International Organization for Standardization (ISO):

'_____ is a management approach for an organization, centered on quality, based on the participation of all its members and aiming at long-term success through customer satisfaction, and benefits to all members of the organization and to society.' ISO 8402:1994

One major aim is to reduce variation from every process so that greater consistency of effort is obtained. (Royse, D., Thyer, B., Padgett D., ' Logan T., 2006)

a. 1990 Clean Air Act
b. Total quality management
c. Quality management
d. 28-hour day

25. _____ is an inventory strategy that strives to improve the return on investment of a business by reducing in-process inventory and its associated carrying costs. To meet _____ objectives, the process relies on signals between different points in the process. This means the process is often driven by a series of signals, or Kanban , which tell production when to make the next part. Kanban are usually 'tickets' but can be simple visual signals, such as the presence or absence of a part on a shelf. Implemented correctly, _____ can dramatically improve a manufacturing organization's return on investment, quality, and efficiency.

# Chapter 1. INTRODUCTION TO OPERATIONS MANAGEMENT

a. 33 Strategies of War
b. 1990 Clean Air Act
c. Just-in-time
d. 28-hour day

26. _____ can be considered to have three main components: quality control, quality assurance and quality improvement. _____ is focused not only on product quality, but also the means to achieve it. _____ therefore uses quality assurance and control of processes as well as products to achieve more consistent quality.

a. Quality management
b. 1990 Clean Air Act
c. Total quality management
d. 28-hour day

27. A _____ or business method is a collection of related, structured activities or tasks that produce a specific service or product (serve a particular goal) for a particular customer or customers. It often can be visualized with a flowchart as a sequence of activities.

There are three types of _____ es:

1. Management processes, the processes that govern the operation of a system. Typical management processes include 'Corporate Governance' and 'Strategic Management'.
2. Operational processes, processes that constitute the core business and create the primary value stream. Typical operational processes are Purchasing, Manufacturing, Marketing, and Sales.
3. Supporting processes, which support the core processes. Examples include Accounting, Recruitment, Technical support.

A _____ begins with a customer's need and ends with a customer's need fulfillment. Process oriented organizations break down the barriers of structural departments and try to avoid functional silos.

a. 33 Strategies of War
b. 1990 Clean Air Act
c. Business process
d. 28-hour day

28. _____ is, in computer science and management, an approach aiming at improvements by means of elevating efficiency and effectiveness of the business process that exist within and across organizations. The key to _____ is for organizations to look at their business processes from a 'clean slate' perspective and determine how they can best construct these processes to improve how they conduct business. _____ Cycle.

## Chapter 1. INTRODUCTION TO OPERATIONS MANAGEMENT

_____ is also known as _____, Business Process Redesign, Business Transformation, or Business Process Change Management.

a. Horizontal integration
b. Personal management interview
c. Product life cycle
d. Business process reengineering


29. _____, in marketing, manufacturing, call centres and management, is the use of flexible computer-aided manufacturing systems to produce custom output. Those systems combine the low unit costs of mass production processes with the flexibility of individual customization.

'_____' is the new frontier in business competition for both manufacturing and service industries.

a. Mass customization
b. 33 Strategies of War
c. 28-hour day
d. 1990 Clean Air Act


30. _____ is the management of a network of interconnected businesses involved in the ultimate provision of product and service packages required by end customers (Harland, 1996.) _____ spans all movement and storage of raw materials, work-in-process inventory, and finished goods from point of origin to point of consumption (supply chain.)

The definition an American professional association put forward is that _____ encompasses the planning and management of all activities involved in sourcing, procurement, conversion, and logistics management activities.

a. Packaging
b. Freight forwarder
c. Drop shipping
d. Supply chain management


31. _____ describes commerce transactions between businesses, such as between a manufacturer and a wholesaler, or between a wholesaler and a retailer. Contrasting terms are business-to-consumer (B2C) and business-to-government (B2G.)

The volume of B2B transactions is much higher than the volume of B2C transactions.

a. Market environment
b. Category management
c. Product bundling
d. Business-to-business

32. Business-to-consumer describes activities of businesses serving end consumers with products and/or services.

An example of a _____ transaction would be a person buying a pair of shoes from a retailer. The transactions that led to the shoes being available for purchase, that is the purchase of the leather, laces, rubber, etc.

a. Green marketing
b. B2C
c. PEST analysis
d. Market environment

33. An _____ is the negative aspects of human activity on the biophysical environment. Environmentalism, a social and environmental movement that started in the 1960s, focuses on addressing _____s through advocacy, education and activism.

Major current _____s are climate change, pollution and resource depletion.

a. Environmental issue
b. A Stake in the Outcome
c. AAAI
d. A4e

34. _____ is a type of trade policy that allows traders to act and transact without interference from government. Thus, the policy permits trading partners mutual gains from trade, with goods and services produced according to the theory of comparative advantage.

Under a _____ policy, prices are a reflection of true supply and demand, and are the sole determinant of resource allocation.

a. 1990 Clean Air Act
b. 33 Strategies of War
c. Free Trade
d. 28-hour day

## Chapter 1. INTRODUCTION TO OPERATIONS MANAGEMENT

35. _____ is a designated group of countries that have agreed to eliminate tariffs, quotas and preferences on most (if not all) goods and services traded between them. It can be considered the second stage of economic integration. Countries choose this kind of economic integration form if their economical structures are complementary.
   a. Free trade area
   b. 33 Strategies of War
   c. 28-hour day
   d. 1990 Clean Air Act

36. The _____ was the outcome of the failure of negotiating governments to create the International Trade Organization (ITO.) GATT was formed in 1947 and lasted until 1994, when it was replaced by the World Trade Organization. The Bretton Woods Conference had introduced the idea for an organization to regulate trade as part of a larger plan for economic recovery after World War II.
   a. Multilateral treaty
   b. 28-hour day
   c. 1990 Clean Air Act
   d. General Agreement on Tariffs and Trade

37. The _____ is a trilateral trade bloc in North America created by the governments of the United States, Canada, and Mexico. The agreement creating the trade bloc came into force on January 1, 1994. It superseded the Canada-United States Free Trade Agreement between the U.S. and Canada.
   a. Trade union
   b. Career portfolios
   c. Business war game
   d. North American Free Trade Agreement

38. _____ is subcontracting a process, such as product design or manufacturing, to a third-party company. The decision to outsource is often made in the interest of lowering cost or making better use of time and energy costs, redirecting or conserving energy directed at the competencies of a particular business, or to make more efficient use of land, labor, capital, (information) technology and resources. _____ became part of the business lexicon during the 1980s.
   a. Opinion leadership
   b. Operant conditioning
   c. Unemployment insurance
   d. Outsourcing

## Chapter 1. INTRODUCTION TO OPERATIONS MANAGEMENT

39. _____ consists of the processes a company uses to track and organize its contacts with its current and prospective customers. _____ software is used to support these processes; information about customers and customer interactions can be entered, stored and accessed by employees in different company departments. Typical _____ goals are to improve services provided to customers, and to use customer contact information for targeted marketing.
   a. Disruptive technology
   b. Green marketing
   c. Marketing plan
   d. Customer relationship management


40. _____ is an integrated communications-based process through which individuals and communities discover that existing and newly-identified needs and wants may be satisfied by the products and services of others.

_____ is defined by the American _____ Association as the activity, set of institutions, and processes for creating, communicating, delivering, and exchanging offerings that have value for customers, clients, partners, and society at large. The term developed from the original meaning which referred literally to going to market, as in shopping, or going to a market to buy or sell goods or services.

   a. Marketing
   b. Disruptive technology
   c. Market development
   d. Customer relationship management


41. _____ is an operational activity which does an aggregate plan for the production process, in advance of 2 to 18 months, to give an idea to management as to what quantity of materials and other resources are to be procured and when, so that the total cost of operations of the organization is kept to the minimum over that period.

The quantity of outsourcing, subcontracting of items, overtime of labor, numbers to be hired and fired in each period and the amount of inventory to be held in stock and to be backlogged for each period are decided. All of these activities are done within the framework of the company ethics, policies, and long term commitment to the society, community and the country of operation.

   a. Aggregate planning
   b. A Stake in the Outcome
   c. Earned Schedule
   d. Earned value management

42. _____ is an increasingly broadening term with which an organization, or other human system describes the combination of traditionally administrative personnel functions with acquisition and application of skills, knowledge and experience, Employee Relations and resource planning at various levels. The field draws upon concepts developed in Industrial/Organizational Psychology and System Theory. _____ has at least two related interpretations depending on context. The original usage derives from political economy and economics, where it was traditionally called labor, one of four factors of production although this perspective is changing as a function of new and ongoing research into more strategic approaches at national levels. This first usage is used more in terms of '_____ development', and can go beyond just organizations to the level of nations . The more traditional usage within corporations and businesses refers to the individuals within a firm or agency, and to the portion of the organization that deals with hiring, firing, training, and other personnel issues, typically referred to as `_____ management'.
   a. Progressive discipline
   b. Human resource management
   c. Human resources
   d. Bradford Factor

# Chapter 2. OPERATIONS STRATEGY AND COMPETITIVENESS

1. _____ refers to the aggregated strategies of single business firm or a strategic business unit (SBU) in a diversified corporation. According to Michael Porter, a firm must formulate a _____ that incorporates either cost leadership, differentiation or focus in order to achieve a sustainable competitive advantage and long-term success in its chosen arenas or industries.

Functional strategies include marketing strategies, new product development strategies, human resource strategies, financial strategies, legal strategies, supply-chain strategies, and information technology management strategies.

   a. Strategic thinking
   b. Competitive heterogeneity
   c. Switching cost
   d. Business strategy


2. _____ is an area of business concerned with the production of goods and services, and involves the responsibility of ensuring that business operations are efficient in terms of using as little resource as needed, and effective in terms of meeting customer requirements. It is concerned with managing the process that converts inputs (in the forms of materials, labour and energy) into outputs (in the form of goods and services.)

Operations traditionally refers to the production of goods and services separately, although the distinction between these two main types of operations is increasingly difficult to make as manufacturers tend to merge product and service offerings.

   a. AAAI
   b. Operations management
   c. A4e
   d. A Stake in the Outcome


3. _____ refers to metrics and measures of output from production processes, per unit of input. Labor _____, for example, is typically measured as a ratio of output per labor-hour, an input. _____ may be conceived of as a metrics of the technical or engineering efficiency of production.
   a. Value engineering
   b. Remanufacturing
   c. Master production schedule
   d. Productivity


4. _____ is something that a firm can do well and that meets the following three conditions:

Competencies are things that companys execute well across several business units or product sectors.

## Chapter 2. OPERATIONS STRATEGY AND COMPETITIVENESS

Firms usually have few competencies, but these are usually less liable to change rapidly.

1. It provides consumer benefits
2. It is not easy for competitors to imitate
3. It can be leveraged widely to many products and markets.

A _____ can take various forms, including technical/subject matter know-how, a reliable process and/or close relationships with customers and suppliers (Mascarenhas et al. 1998.)

   a. Learning-by-doing
   b. Core competency
   c. NAIRU
   d. Dominant Design


5. A _____ is a brief written statement of the purpose of a company or organization. Ideally, a _____ guides the actions of the organization, spells out its overall goal, provides a sense of direction, and guides decision making for all levels of management.

_____s often contain the following:

- Purpose and aim of the organization
- The organization's primary stakeholders: clients, stockholders, etc.
- Responsibilities of the organization toward these stakeholders
- Products and services offered

In developing a _____:

- Encourage as much input as feasible from employees, volunteers, and other stakeholders
- Publicize it broadly

The _____ can be used to resolve differences between business stakeholders. Stakeholders include: employees including managers and executives, stockholders, board of directors, customers, suppliers, distributors, creditors, governments (local, state, federal, etc.), unions, competitors, NGO's, and the general public.

   a. Mission statement
   b. 1990 Clean Air Act
   c. 28-hour day
   d. 33 Strategies of War

## Chapter 2. OPERATIONS STRATEGY AND COMPETITIVENESS

6. _____ is a process of gathering, analyzing, and dispensing information for tactical or strategic purposes. The _____ process entails obtaining both factual and subjective information on the business environments in which a company is operating or considering entering.

There are three ways of scanning the business environment:

- Ad-hoc scanning - Short term, infrequent examinations usually initiated by a crisis
- Regular scanning - Studies done on a regular schedule (say, once a year)
- Continuous scanning(also called continuous learning) - continuous structured data collection and processing on a broad range of environmental factors

Most commentators feel that in today's turbulent business environment the best scanning method available is continuous scanning. This allows the firm to :

-act quickly-take advantage of opportunities before competitors do-respond to environmental threats before significant damage is done

   a. A4e
   b. A Stake in the Outcome
   c. Environmental scanning
   d. AAAI

7. The term '_____' refers to the concept of collecting information and attempting to spot a pattern in the information. In some fields of study, the term '_____' has more formally-defined meanings.

In project management _____ is a mathematical technique that uses historical results to predict future outcome.

   a. Regression analysis
   b. Least squares
   c. Trend analysis
   d. Stepwise regression

8. A _____ is a formal relationship between two or more parties to pursue a set of agreed upon goals or to meet a critical business need while remaining independent organizations.

Partners may provide the _____ with resources such as products, distribution channels, manufacturing capability, project funding, capital equipment, knowledge, expertise, or intellectual property. The alliance is a cooperation or collaboration which aims for a synergy where each partner hopes that the benefits from the alliance will be greater than those from individual efforts.

## Chapter 2. OPERATIONS STRATEGY AND COMPETITIVENESS       17

   a. Farmshoring
   b. Process automation
   c. Strategic alliance
   d. Golden parachute



9.  A _____ is a formal statement of a set of business goals, the reasons why they are believed attainable, and the plan for reaching those goals. It may also contain background information about the organization or team attempting to reach those goals.

The business goals may be defined for for-profit or for non-profit organizations.

   a. Time management
   b. Crisis management
   c. Distributed management
   d. Business plan



10. In economics, business, retail, and accounting, a _____ is the value of money that has been used up to produce something, and hence is not available for use anymore. In economics, a _____ is an alternative that is given up as a result of a decision. In business, the _____ may be one of acquisition, in which case the amount of money expended to acquire it is counted as _____.
   a. Cost allocation
   b. Fixed costs
   c. Cost overrun
   d. Cost



11. _____ in its literal sense is the process of transformation of local or regional phenomena into global ones. It can be described as a process by which the people of the world are unified into a single society and function together.

This process is a combination of economic, technological, sociocultural and political forces.

   a. Globalization
   b. Histogram
   c. Collaborative Planning, Forecasting and Replenishment
   d. Cost Management



12. _____ is an advertisement in which a particular product specifically mentions a competitor by name for the express purpose of showing why the competitor is inferior to the product naming it.

This should not be confused with parody advertisements, where a fictional product is being advertised for the purpose of poking fun at the particular advertisement, nor should it be confused with the use of a coined brand name for the purpose of comparing the product without actually naming an actual competitor. ('Wikipedia tastes better and is less filling than the Encyclopedia Galactica.')

In the 1980s, during what has been referred to as the cola wars, soft-drink manufacturer Pepsi ran a series of advertisements where people, caught on hidden camera, in a blind taste test, chose Pepsi over rival Coca-Cola.

   a. Comparative advertising
   b. 1990 Clean Air Act
   c. 33 Strategies of War
   d. 28-hour day


13. _____ measures the changes in output per unit of combined inputs. Indexes of MFP are produced for the private business, private nonfarm business, and manufacturing sectors of the economy. MFP is also developed for 2-and 3-digit Standard Industrial Classification (SIC) thru 1987, and NAICS (North Atlantic Industrial Classification System) thru 2005 for manufacturing industries, the railroad transportation industry, the air transportation industry, and the utility and gas industry.
   a. Production function
   b. Diseconomies of scale
   c. Multifactor productivity
   d. Factors of production


14. In economics, the _____ is a subset of the domestic economy excluding the economic activities of general government, private households, and nonprofit organizations serving individuals. In the United States the _____ accounted for about 78 percent of the value of gross domestic product (GDP) in 2000. .
   a. Choquet integral
   b. Long term investment plan
   c. Private placement
   d. Business sector


15. _____ is an integrated communications-based process through which individuals and communities discover that existing and newly-identified needs and wants may be satisfied by the products and services of others.

_____ is defined by the American _____ Association as the activity, set of institutions, and processes for creating, communicating, delivering, and exchanging offerings that have value for customers, clients, partners, and society at large. The term developed from the original meaning which referred literally to going to market, as in shopping, or going to a market to buy or sell goods or services.

a. Customer relationship management
b. Market development
c. Marketing
d. Disruptive technology

16. A _____ is the system of organizations, people, technology, activities, information and resources involved in moving a product or service from supplier to customer. _____ activities transform natural resources, raw materials and components into a finished product that is delivered to the end customer. In sophisticated _____ systems, used products may re-enter the _____ at any point where residual value is recyclable.

a. Packaging
b. Wholesalers
c. Drop shipping
d. Supply chain

17. _____ is the management of a network of interconnected businesses involved in the ultimate provision of product and service packages required by end customers (Harland, 1996.) _____ spans all movement and storage of raw materials, work-in-process inventory, and finished goods from point of origin to point of consumption (supply chain.)

The definition an American professional association put forward is that _____ encompasses the planning and management of all activities involved in sourcing, procurement, conversion, and logistics management activities.

a. Drop shipping
b. Freight forwarder
c. Packaging
d. Supply chain management

18. _____ is an operational activity which does an aggregate plan for the production process, in advance of 2 to 18 months, to give an idea to management as to what quantity of materials and other resources are to be procured and when, so that the total cost of operations of the organization is kept to the minimum over that period.

The quantity of outsourcing, subcontracting of items, overtime of labor, numbers to be hired and fired in each period and the amount of inventory to be held in stock and to be backlogged for each period are decided. All of these activities are done within the framework of the company ethics, policies, and long term commitment to the society, community and the country of operation.

a. A Stake in the Outcome
b. Earned Schedule
c. Earned value management
d. Aggregate planning

## Chapter 3. PRODUCT DESIGN AND PROCESS SELECTION

1. _____ can be defined as the idea generation, concept development, testing and manufacturing or implementation of a physical object or service. _____ers conceptualize and evaluate ideas, making them tangible through products in a more systematic approach. The role of a _____er encompasses many characteristics of the marketing manager, product manager, industrial designer and design engineer.
   a. Abraham Harold Maslow
   b. Adam Smith
   c. Affiliation
   d. Product design

2. _____ is an advertisement in which a particular product specifically mentions a competitor by name for the express purpose of showing why the competitor is inferior to the product naming it.

   This should not be confused with parody advertisements, where a fictional product is being advertised for the purpose of poking fun at the particular advertisement, nor should it be confused with the use of a coined brand name for the purpose of comparing the product without actually naming an actual competitor. ('Wikipedia tastes better and is less filling than the Encyclopedia Galactica.')

   In the 1980s, during what has been referred to as the cola wars, soft-drink manufacturer Pepsi ran a series of advertisements where people, caught on hidden camera, in a blind taste test, chose Pepsi over rival Coca-Cola.

   a. 1990 Clean Air Act
   b. Comparative advertising
   c. 28-hour day
   d. 33 Strategies of War

3. _____ is the process of comparing the cost, cycle time, productivity, or quality of a specific process or method to another that is widely considered to be an industry standard or best practice. Essentially, _____ provides a snapshot of the performance of your business and helps you understand where you are in relation to a particular standard. The result is often a business case for making changes in order to make improvements.
   a. Competitive heterogeneity
   b. Cost leadership
   c. Complementors
   d. Benchmarking

4. _____ is the process of discovering the technological principles of a device, object or system through analysis of its structure, function and operation. It often involves taking something (e.g., a mechanical device, electronic component, or software program) apart and analyzing its workings in detail to be used in maintenance, or to try to make a new device or program that does the same thing without copying anything from the original.

   _____ has its origins in the analysis of hardware for commercial or military advantage .

## Chapter 3. PRODUCT DESIGN AND PROCESS SELECTION

   a. 1990 Clean Air Act
   b. Predictive maintenance
   c. 28-hour day
   d. Reverse engineering

5. In economics, _____ are business expenses that are not dependent on the activities of the business They tend to be time-related, such as salaries or rents being paid per month. This is in contrast to variable costs, which are volume-related (and are paid per quantity.)

In management accounting, _____ are defined as expenses that do not change in proportion to the activity of a business, within the relevant period or scale of production.

   a. Transaction cost
   b. Cost allocation
   c. Cost of quality
   d. Fixed costs

6. _____ is an integrated communications-based process through which individuals and communities discover that existing and newly-identified needs and wants may be satisfied by the products and services of others.

_____ is defined by the American _____ Association as the activity, set of institutions, and processes for creating, communicating, delivering, and exchanging offerings that have value for customers, clients, partners, and society at large. The term developed from the original meaning which referred literally to going to market, as in shopping, or going to a market to buy or sell goods or services.

   a. Marketing
   b. Customer relationship management
   c. Market development
   d. Disruptive technology

7. _____ is an area of business concerned with the production of goods and services, and involves the responsibility of ensuring that business operations are efficient in terms of using as little resource as needed, and effective in terms of meeting customer requirements. It is concerned with managing the process that converts inputs (in the forms of materials, labour and energy) into outputs (in the form of goods and services.)

Operations traditionally refers to the production of goods and services separately, although the distinction between these two main types of operations is increasingly difficult to make as manufacturers tend to merge product and service offerings.

a. Operations management
b. A4e
c. A Stake in the Outcome
d. AAAI


8. _____ is an operational activity which does an aggregate plan for the production process, in advance of 2 to 18 months, to give an idea to management as to what quantity of materials and other resources are to be procured and when, so that the total cost of operations of the organization is kept to the minimum over that period.

The quantity of outsourcing, subcontracting of items, overtime of labor, numbers to be hired and fired in each period and the amount of inventory to be held in stock and to be backlogged for each period are decided. All of these activities are done within the framework of the company ethics, policies, and long term commitment to the society, community and the country of operation.

a. Aggregate planning
b. Earned value management
c. A Stake in the Outcome
d. Earned Schedule


9. _____ is one of the managerial functions like planning, organizing, staffing and directing. It is an important function because it helps to check the errors and to take the corrective action so that deviation from standards are minimized and stated goals of the organization are achieved in desired manner. According to modern concepts, _____ is a foreseeing action whereas earlier concept of _____ was used only when errors were detected. _____ in management means setting standards, measuring actual performance and taking corrective action.
a. Decision tree pruning
b. Schedule of reinforcement
c. Turnover
d. Control


10. The _____ in statistical process control is a tool used to determine whether a manufacturing or business process is in a state of statistical control or not.

If the chart indicates that the process is currently under control then it can be used with confidence to predict the future performance of the process. If the chart indicates that the process being monitored is not in control, the pattern it reveals can help determine the source of variation to be eliminated to bring the process back into control.

## Chapter 3. PRODUCT DESIGN AND PROCESS SELECTION

a. Time series analysis
b. Control chart
c. Failure rate
d. Simple moving average


11. In economics, business, retail, and accounting, a _____ is the value of money that has been used up to produce something, and hence is not available for use anymore. In economics, a _____ is an alternative that is given up as a result of a decision. In business, the _____ may be one of acquisition, in which case the amount of money expended to acquire it is counted as _____.

   a. Fixed costs
   b. Cost allocation
   c. Cost
   d. Cost overrun


12. _____s are expenses that change in proportion to the activity of a business. In other words, _____ is the sum of marginal costs. It can also be considered normal costs.

   a. Cost overrun
   b. Fixed costs
   c. Cost accounting
   d. Variable cost


13. Marketing research is a form of business research and is generally divided into two categories: consumer _____ and business-to-business (B2B) _____, which was previously known as industrial marketing research. Consumer marketing research studies the buying habits of individual people while business-to-business marketing research investigates the markets for products sold by one business to another.

Consumer _____ is a form of applied sociology that concentrates on understanding the behaviours, whims and preferences, of consumers in a market-based economy, and aims to understand the effects and comparative success of marketing campaigns.

   a. Questionnaire construction
   b. Questionnaire
   c. Market research
   d. Mystery shoppers


14. In mathematical logic, _____ is a valid argument and rule of inference which makes the inference that, if the conjunction A and B is true, then A is true, and B is true.

## Chapter 3. PRODUCT DESIGN AND PROCESS SELECTION

In formal language:

$$A \wedge B \vdash A$$

or

$$A \wedge B \vdash B$$

The argument has one premise, namely a conjunction, and one often uses _____ in longer arguments to derive one of the conjuncts.

An example in English:

It's raining and it's pouring.

a. Validity
b. 1990 Clean Air Act
c. Fuzzy logic
d. Simplification


15. _____ Management is the succession of strategies used by management as a product goes through its _____. The conditions in which a product is sold changes over time and must be managed as it moves through its succession of stages.

The _____ goes through many phases, involves many professional disciplines, and requires many skills, tools and processes.

a. Job hunting
b. Golden handshake
c. Strategic Alliance
d. Product life cycle


16. _____ is a work methodology based on the parallelization of tasks (ie. concurrently.) It refers to an approach used in product development in which functions of design engineering, manufacturing engineering and other functions are integrated to reduce the elapsed time required to bring a new product to the market.

## Chapter 3. PRODUCT DESIGN AND PROCESS SELECTION

a. Work package
b. Project management
c. Concurrent engineering
d. Critical Chain Project Management

17. _____ is the process of disassembly and recovery at the module level and, eventually, at the component level. It requires the repair or replacement of worn out or obsolete components and modules. Parts subject to degradation affecting the performance or the expected life of the whole are replaced.
   a. Methods-time measurement
   b. Remanufacturing
   c. Capacity planning
   d. Productivity

18. In probability theory, a probability distribution is called _____ if its cumulative distribution function is _____. This is equivalent to saying that for random variables X with the distribution in question, Pr[X = a] = 0 for all real numbers a, i.e.: the probability that X attains the value a is zero, for any number a. If the distribution of X is _____ then X is called a _____ random variable.
   a. Connectionist expert systems
   b. Continuous
   c. Decision tree pruning
   d. Pay Band

19. _____ refers to the movement of cash into or out of a business or financial product. It is usually measured during a specified, finite period of time. Measurement of _____ can be used

   - to determine a project's rate of return or value. The time of _____s into and out of projects are used as inputs in financial models such as internal rate of return, and net present value.
   - to determine problems with a business's liquidity. Being profitable does not necessarily mean being liquid. A company can fail because of a shortage of cash, even while profitable.
   - as an alternate measure of a business's profits when it is believed that accrual accounting concepts do not represent economic realities. For example, a company may be notionally profitable but generating little operational cash (as may be the case for a company that barters its products rather than selling for cash.) In such a case, the company may be deriving additional operating cash by issuing shares evaluating default risk, re-investment requirements, etc.

_____ is a generic term used differently depending on the context. It may be defined by users for their own purposes.

## Chapter 3. PRODUCT DESIGN AND PROCESS SELECTION

a. Cash flow
b. Sweat equity
c. Gross profit
d. Gross profit margin


20. A _____ is a common type of chart, that represents an algorithm or process, showing the steps as boxes of various kinds, and their order by connecting these with arrows. _____s are used in analyzing, designing, documenting or managing a process or program in various fields.

The first structured method for documenting process flow, the 'flow process chart', was introduced by Frank Gilbreth to members of ASME in 1921 as the presentation 'Process Charts--First Steps in Finding the One Best Way'.

a. 28-hour day
b. 33 Strategies of War
c. 1990 Clean Air Act
d. Flowchart


21. _____ refers to metrics and measures of output from production processes, per unit of input. Labor _____, for example, is typically measured as a ratio of output per labor-hour, an input. _____ may be conceived of as a metrics of the technical or engineering efficiency of production.
a. Remanufacturing
b. Value engineering
c. Master production schedule
d. Productivity


22. In queueing theory, _____ is the proportion of the system's resources which is used by the traffic which arrives at it. It should be strictly less than one for the system to function well. It is usually represented by the symbol ρ.
a. Utilization
b. A Stake in the Outcome
c. AAAI
d. A4e


23. In economics, _____ is the desire to own something and the ability to pay for it. The term _____ signifies the ability or the willingness to buy a particular commodity at a given point of time.

## Chapter 3. PRODUCT DESIGN AND PROCESS SELECTION

a. 1990 Clean Air Act
b. 33 Strategies of War
c. Demand
d. 28-hour day

24. _____ can be regarded as an outcome of mental processes (cognitive process) leading to the selection of a course of action among several alternatives. Every _____ process produces a final choice. The output can be an action or an opinion of choice.
   a. Decision making
   b. 33 Strategies of War
   c. 28-hour day
   d. 1990 Clean Air Act

25. In microeconomics and management, the term _____ describes a style of management control. Vertically integrated companies are united through a hierarchy with a common owner. Usually each member of the hierarchy produces a different product or (market-specific) service, and the products combine to satisfy a common need.
   a. 28-hour day
   b. 1990 Clean Air Act
   c. Vertical integration
   d. 33 Strategies of War

26. _____ is used for the design, development, analysis, and optimization of technical processes and is mainly applied to chemical plants and chemical processes, but also to power stations, and similar technical facilities. Process flow diagram of a typical amine treating process used in industrial plants

_____ is a model-based representation of chemical, physical, biological, and other technical processes and unit operations in software. Basic prerequisites are a thorough knowledge of chemical and physical properties of pure components and mixtures, of reactions, and of mathematical models which, in combination, allow the calculation of a process in computers.

   a. 28-hour day
   b. 33 Strategies of War
   c. 1990 Clean Air Act
   d. Process simulation

## Chapter 3. PRODUCT DESIGN AND PROCESS SELECTION

27. _____ is the use of control systems (such as numerical control, programmable logic control, and other industrial control systems), in concert with other applications of information technology (such as computer-aided technologies [CAD, CAM, CAx]), to control industrial machinery and processes, reducing the need for human intervention. In the scope of industrialization, _____ is a step beyond mechanization. Whereas mechanization provided human operators with machinery to assist them with the physical requirements of work, _____ greatly reduces the need for human sensory and mental requirements as well.

   a. AAAI
   b. A4e
   c. A Stake in the Outcome
   d. Automation


28. _____ is the use of an object (typically referred to as an RFID tag) applied to or incorporated into a product, animal, or person for the purpose of identification and tracking using radio waves. Some tags can be read from several meters away and beyond the line of sight of the reader.

Most RFID tags contain at least two parts.

   a. 33 Strategies of War
   b. 1990 Clean Air Act
   c. Radio-frequency identification
   d. 28-hour day


29. In marketing, _____ has come to mean the process by which marketers try to create an image or identity in the minds of their target market for its product, brand, or organization. It is the 'relative competitive comparison' their product occupies in a given market as perceived by the target market.

Re-_____ involves changing the identity of a product, relative to the identity of competing products, in the collective minds of the target market.

   a. PEST analysis
   b. Customer analytics
   c. Context analysis
   d. Positioning


30. A _____ system is a manufacturing system in which there is some amount of flexibility that allows the system to react in the case of changes, whether predicted or unpredicted. This flexibility is generally considered to fall into two categories, which both contain numerous subcategories.

The first category, machine flexibility, covers the system's ability to be changed to produce new product types, and ability to change the order of operations executed on a part. The second category is called routing flexibility, which consists of the ability to use multiple machines to perform the same operation on a part, as well as the system's ability to absorb large-scale changes, such as in volume, capacity, or capability.

a. Jidoka
b. Homeworkers
c. Flexible manufacturing
d. Manufacturing resource planning


31. _____ is the use of information technology to support engineers in tasks such as analysis, simulation, design, manufacture, planning, diagnosis, and repair.

Software tools that have been developed to support these activities are considered CAE tools. CAE tools are being used, for example, to analyze the robustness and performance of components and assemblies.

a. 33 Strategies of War
b. 28-hour day
c. 1990 Clean Air Act
d. Computer-aided engineering


32. A _____ is the system of organizations, people, technology, activities, information and resources involved in moving a product or service from supplier to customer. _____ activities transform natural resources, raw materials and components into a finished product that is delivered to the end customer. In sophisticated _____ systems, used products may re-enter the _____ at any point where residual value is recyclable.

a. Wholesalers
b. Drop shipping
c. Supply chain
d. Packaging


33. The _____ captures an expanded spectrum of values and criteria for measuring organizational success: economic, ecological and social. With the ratification of the United Nations and ICLEI _____ standard for urban and community accounting in early 2007, this became the dominant approach to public sector full cost accounting. Similar UN standards apply to natural capital and human capital measurement to assist in measurements required by _____, e.g. the ecoBudget standard for reporting ecological footprint.

## Chapter 3. PRODUCT DESIGN AND PROCESS SELECTION

a. 33 Strategies of War
b. 28-hour day
c. 1990 Clean Air Act
d. Triple bottom line


34. _____ is an increasingly broadening term with which an organization, or other human system describes the combination of traditionally administrative personnel functions with acquisition and application of skills, knowledge and experience, Employee Relations and resource planning at various levels. The field draws upon concepts developed in Industrial/Organizational Psychology and System Theory. _____ has at least two related interpretations depending on context. The original usage derives from political economy and economics, where it was traditionally called labor, one of four factors of production although this perspective is changing as a function of new and ongoing research into more strategic approaches at national levels. This first usage is used more in terms of '_____ development', and can go beyond just organizations to the level of nations . The more traditional usage within corporations and businesses refers to the individuals within a firm or agency, and to the portion of the organization that deals with hiring, firing, training, and other personnel issues, typically referred to as `_____ management'.
   a. Bradford Factor
   b. Human resource management
   c. Progressive discipline
   d. Human resources


35. _____ is the management of a network of interconnected businesses involved in the ultimate provision of product and service packages required by end customers (Harland, 1996.) _____ spans all movement and storage of raw materials, work-in-process inventory, and finished goods from point of origin to point of consumption (supply chain.)

The definition an American professional association put forward is that _____ encompasses the planning and management of all activities involved in sourcing, procurement, conversion, and logistics management activities.

   a. Supply chain management
   b. Packaging
   c. Freight forwarder
   d. Drop shipping


36. _____ is an inventory strategy that strives to improve the return on investment of a business by reducing in-process inventory and its associated carrying costs. To meet _____ objectives, the process relies on signals between different points in the process. This means the process is often driven by a series of signals, or Kanban , which tell production when to make the next part. Kanban are usually 'tickets' but can be simple visual signals, such as the presence or absence of a part on a shelf. Implemented correctly, _____ can dramatically improve a manufacturing organization's return on investment, quality, and efficiency.

a. Just-in-time
b. 1990 Clean Air Act
c. 33 Strategies of War
d. 28-hour day

## Chapter 4. SUPPLY CHAIN MANAGEMENT

1. A _____ is the system of organizations, people, technology, activities, information and resources involved in moving a product or service from supplier to customer. _____ activities transform natural resources, raw materials and components into a finished product that is delivered to the end customer. In sophisticated _____ systems, used products may re-enter the _____ at any point where residual value is recyclable.
   a. Drop shipping
   b. Supply chain
   c. Wholesalers
   d. Packaging

2. _____ is the management of a network of interconnected businesses involved in the ultimate provision of product and service packages required by end customers (Harland, 1996.) _____ spans all movement and storage of raw materials, work-in-process inventory, and finished goods from point of origin to point of consumption (supply chain.)

   The definition an American professional association put forward is that _____ encompasses the planning and management of all activities involved in sourcing, procurement, conversion, and logistics management activities.

   a. Packaging
   b. Freight forwarder
   c. Drop shipping
   d. Supply chain management

3. A _____ is a list of the general tasks and responsibilities of a position. Typically, it also includes to whom the position reports, specifications such as the qualifications needed by the person in the job, salary range for the position, etc. A _____ is usually developed by conducting a job analysis, which includes examining the tasks and sequences of tasks necessary to perform the job.
   a. Recruitment Process Insourcing
   b. Recruitment advertising
   c. Job description
   d. Recruitment

4. The _____ is an observed phenomenon in forecast-driven distribution channels. The concept has its roots in J Forrester's Industrial Dynamics (1961) and thus it is also known as the Forrester Effect. Since the oscillating demand magnification upstream a supply chain reminds someone of a cracking whip it became famous as the _____.
   a. 1990 Clean Air Act
   b. 33 Strategies of War
   c. 28-hour day
   d. Bullwhip effect

5. _____ is one of the four elements of marketing mix. An organization or set of organizations (go-betweens) involved in the process of making a product or service available for use or consumption by a consumer or business user.

The other three parts of the marketing mix are product, pricing, and promotion.

 a. Matching theory
 b. Missing completely at random
 c. Job creation programs
 d. Distribution

6. _____ is the management of the flow of goods, information and other resources, including energy and people, between the point of origin and the point of consumption in order to meet the requirements of consumers (frequently, and originally, military organizations.) _____ involves the integration of information, transportation, inventory, warehousing, material-handling, and packaging, and occasionally security. _____ is a channel of the supply chain which adds the value of time and place utility.
 a. Third-party logistics
 b. Logistics
 c. 28-hour day
 d. 1990 Clean Air Act

7. In economics, _____ is the desire to own something and the ability to pay for it. The term _____ signifies the ability or the willingness to buy a particular commodity at a given point of time.
 a. Demand
 b. 28-hour day
 c. 33 Strategies of War
 d. 1990 Clean Air Act

8. _____ describes commerce transactions between businesses, such as between a manufacturer and a wholesaler, or between a wholesaler and a retailer. Contrasting terms are business-to-consumer (B2C) and business-to-government (B2G.)

The volume of B2B transactions is much higher than the volume of B2C transactions.

 a. Market environment
 b. Product bundling
 c. Business-to-business
 d. Category management

## Chapter 4. SUPPLY CHAIN MANAGEMENT

9. _____ refers to the structured transmission of data between organizations by electronic means. It is used to transfer electronic documents from one computer system to another (ie) from one trading partner to another trading partner. It is more than mere E-mail; for instance, organizations might replace bills of lading and even checks with appropriate _____ messages.
   a. A4e
   b. AAAI
   c. Electronic data interchange
   d. A Stake in the Outcome

10. _____, commonly known as e-commerce, consists of the buying and selling of products or services over electronic systems such as the Internet and other computer networks. The amount of trade conducted electronically has grown extraordinarily with widespread Internet usage. The use of commerce is conducted in this way, spurring and drawing on innovations in electronic funds transfer, supply chain management, Internet marketing, online transaction processing, electronic data interchange (EDI), inventory management systems, and automated data collection systems.
    a. A4e
    b. A Stake in the Outcome
    c. Online shopping
    d. Electronic Commerce

11. Business-to-consumer describes activities of businesses serving end consumers with products and/or services.

An example of a _____ transaction would be a person buying a pair of shoes from a retailer. The transactions that led to the shoes being available for purchase, that is the purchase of the leather, laces, rubber, etc.

   a. Market environment
   b. B2C
   c. PEST analysis
   d. Green marketing

12. _____ is a form of communication that typically attempts to persuade potential customers to purchase or to consume more of a particular brand of product or service. 'While now central to the contemporary global economy and the reproduction of global production networks, it is only quite recently that _____ has been more than a marginal influence on patterns of sales and production. The formation of modern _____ was intimately bound up with the emergence of new forms of monopoly capitalism around the end of the 19th and beginning of the 20th century as one element in corporate strategies to create, organize and where possible control markets, especially for mass produced consumer goods.

a. Advertising
b. A Stake in the Outcome
c. AAAI
d. A4e

13. _____ is the process of determining the production capacity needed by an organization to meet changing demands for its products. In the context of _____, 'capacity' is the maximum amount of work that an organization is capable of completing in a given period of time.

A discrepancy between the capacity of an organization and the demands of its customers results in inefficiency, either in under-utilized resources or unfulfilled customers.

a. Productivity
b. Capacity planning
c. Remanufacturing
d. Scientific management

14. _____ is a broad label that refers to any individuals or households that use goods and services generated within the economy. The concept of a _____ is used in different contexts, so that the usage and significance of the term may vary.

Typically when business people and economists talk of _____s they are talking about person as _____, an aggregated commodity item with little individuality other than that expressed in the buy/not-buy decision.

a. 1990 Clean Air Act
b. 28-hour day
c. 33 Strategies of War
d. Consumer

15. An _____ is a private network that uses Internet protocols, network connectivity, and possibly the public telecommunication system to securely share part of an organization's information or operations with suppliers, vendors, partners, customers or other businesses. An _____ can be viewed as part of a company's intranet that is extended to users outside the company (e.g.: normally over the Internet.) It has also been described as a 'state of mind' in which the Internet is perceived as a way to do business with a preapproved set of other companies business-to-business (B2B), in isolation from all other Internet users.

a. A Stake in the Outcome
b. AAAI
c. A4e
d. Extranet



16. An _____ is a private computer network that uses Internet technologies to securely share any part of an organization's information or operational systems with its employees. Sometimes the term refers only to the organization's internal website, but often it is a more extensive part of the organization's computer infrastructure and private websites are an important component and focal point of internal communication and collaboration.

An _____ is built from the same concepts and technologies used for the Internet, such as client-server computing and the Internet Protocol Suite (TCP/IP.)

a. A Stake in the Outcome
b. AAAI
c. A4e
d. Intranet



17. _____ in its literal sense is the process of transformation of local or regional phenomena into global ones. It can be described as a process by which the people of the world are unified into a single society and function together.

This process is a combination of economic, technological, sociocultural and political forces.

a. Globalization
b. Collaborative Planning, Forecasting and Replenishment
c. Histogram
d. Cost Management



18. _____ is an advertisement in which a particular product specifically mentions a competitor by name for the express purpose of showing why the competitor is inferior to the product naming it.

This should not be confused with parody advertisements, where a fictional product is being advertised for the purpose of poking fun at the particular advertisement, nor should it be confused with the use of a coined brand name for the purpose of comparing the product without actually naming an actual competitor. ('Wikipedia tastes better and is less filling than the Encyclopedia Galactica.')

In the 1980s, during what has been referred to as the cola wars, soft-drink manufacturer Pepsi ran a series of advertisements where people, caught on hidden camera, in a blind taste test, chose Pepsi over rival Coca-Cola.

## Chapter 4. SUPPLY CHAIN MANAGEMENT

   a. Comparative advertising
   b. 33 Strategies of War
   c. 28-hour day
   d. 1990 Clean Air Act

19. _____ is the science, art and technology of enclosing or protecting products for distribution, storage, sale, and use. _____ also refers to the process of design, evaluation, and production of packages. _____ can be described as a coordinated system of preparing goods for transport, warehousing, logistics, sale, and end use.
   a. Wholesalers
   b. Supply chain management
   c. Supply chain
   d. Packaging

20. The _____ is a systematic, interactive forecasting method which relies on a panel of independent experts. The carefully selected experts answer questionnaires in two or more rounds. After each round, a facilitator provides an anonymous summary of the experts' forecasts from the previous round as well as the reasons they provided for their judgments.
   a. Hoshin Kanri
   b. Quality function deployment
   c. Learning organization
   d. Delphi method

21. In finance, the _____s between two currencies specifies how much one currency is worth in terms of the other. It is the value of a foreign nation's currency in terms of the home nation's currency. For example an _____ of 102 Japanese yen to the United States dollar means that JPY 102 is worth the same as USD 1.
   a. AAAI
   b. Exchange rate
   c. A Stake in the Outcome
   d. A4e

22. In the fields of science, engineering, industry and statistics, _____ is the degree of closeness of a measured or calculated quantity to its actual (true) value. _____ is closely related to precision, also called reproducibility or repeatability, the degree to which further measurements or calculations show the same or similar results. _____ indicates proximity to the true value, precision to the repeatability or reproducibility of the measurement

The results of calculations or a measurement can be accurate but not precise, precise but not accurate, neither, or both.

## Chapter 4. SUPPLY CHAIN MANAGEMENT

a. A4e
b. A Stake in the Outcome
c. AAAI
d. Accuracy

23. _____ is the process of estimation in unknown situations. Prediction is a similar, but more general term. Both can refer to estimation of time series, cross-sectional or longitudinal data.

 a. 33 Strategies of War
 b. 1990 Clean Air Act
 c. Forecasting
 d. 28-hour day

24. A _____ is the period of time between the initiation of any process of production and the completion of that process. Thus the _____ for ordering a new car from a manufacturer may be anywhere from 2 weeks to 6 months. In industry, _____ reduction is an important part of lean manufacturing.

 a. Lead time
 b. 28-hour day
 c. 1990 Clean Air Act
 d. 33 Strategies of War

25. The term '_____' refers to the concept of collecting information and attempting to spot a pattern in the information. In some fields of study, the term '_____' has more formally-defined meanings.

In project management _____ is a mathematical technique that uses historical results to predict future outcome.

 a. Least squares
 b. Regression analysis
 c. Stepwise regression
 d. Trend analysis

26. _____ is subcontracting a process, such as product design or manufacturing, to a third-party company. The decision to outsource is often made in the interest of lowering cost or making better use of time and energy costs, redirecting or conserving energy directed at the competencies of a particular business, or to make more efficient use of land, labor, capital, (information) technology and resources. _____ became part of the business lexicon during the 1980s.

a. Unemployment insurance
b. Outsourcing
c. Opinion leadership
d. Operant conditioning

27. In business, the term word _____ refers to a number of procurement practices, aimed at finding, evaluating and engaging suppliers of goods and services:

- Global _____, a procurement strategy aimed at exploiting global efficiencies in production
- Strategic _____, a component of supply chain management, for improving and re-evaluating purchasing activities
- _____, the identification of job candidates through proactive recruiting technique
- Co-_____, a type of auditing service
- Low-cost country _____, a procurement strategy for acquiring materials from countries with lower labour and production costs in order to cut operating expenses
- Corporate _____, a supply chain, purchasing/procurement, and inventory function
- Second-tier _____, a practice of rewarding suppliers for attempting to achieve minority-owned business spending goals of their customer
- Netsourcing, a practice of utilizing an established group of businesses, individuals, or hardware ' software applications to streamline or initiate procurement practices by tapping in to and working through a third party provider
- Inverted _____, a price volatility reduction strategy usually conducted by procurement or supply-chain person by which the value of an organization's waste-stream is maximized by actively seeking out the highest price possible from a range of potential buyers exploiting price trends and other market factors
- Multisourcing, a strategy that treats a given function, such as IT, as a portfolio of activities, some of which should be outsourced and others of which should be performed by internal staff.
- Crowdsourcing, using an undefined, generally large group of people or community in the form of an open call to perform a task

In journalism, it can also refer to:

- Journalism _____, the practice of identifying a person or publication that gives information
- Single _____, the reuse of content in publishing

In computing, it can refer to:

- Open-_____, the act of releasing previously proprietary software under an open source/free software license
- Power _____ equipment, network devices that will provide power in a Power over Ethernet (PoE) setup

*Chapter 4. SUPPLY CHAIN MANAGEMENT* 41

   a. Cost Management
   b. Continuous
   c. Sourcing
   d. Reinforcement

28. In microeconomics and management, the term _____ describes a style of management control. Vertically integrated companies are united through a hierarchy with a common owner. Usually each member of the hierarchy produces a different product or (market-specific) service, and the products combine to satisfy a common need.

   a. 28-hour day
   b. 1990 Clean Air Act
   c. 33 Strategies of War
   d. Vertical integration

29. _____ can be defined as the idea generation, concept development, testing and manufacturing or implementation of a physical object or service. _____ers conceptualize and evaluate ideas, making them tangible through products in a more systematic approach. The role of a _____er encompasses many characteristics of the marketing manager, product manager, industrial designer and design engineer.

   a. Product design
   b. Adam Smith
   c. Affiliation
   d. Abraham Harold Maslow

30. The _____ is a not-for-profit United States association for the benefit of the purchasing and supply management profession, particularly in the areas of education and research.

It was founded in 1913 as the New York Association of Purchasing Management after a purchasing meeting organized by the Thomas Register. It was established in 1915 as the National Association of Purchasing Management.

   a. AAAI
   b. Institute for Supply Management
   c. A4e
   d. A Stake in the Outcome

## Chapter 4. SUPPLY CHAIN MANAGEMENT

31. _____ is an inventory strategy that strives to improve the return on investment of a business by reducing in-process inventory and its associated carrying costs. To meet _____ objectives, the process relies on signals between different points in the process. This means the process is often driven by a series of signals, or Kanban , which tell production when to make the next part. Kanban are usually 'tickets' but can be simple visual signals, such as the presence or absence of a part on a shelf. Implemented correctly, _____ can dramatically improve a manufacturing organization's return on investment, quality, and efficiency.
   a. Just-in-time
   b. 1990 Clean Air Act
   c. 28-hour day
   d. 33 Strategies of War

32. A _____ is a commercial building for storage of goods. _____s are used by manufacturers, importers, exporters, wholesalers, transport businesses, customs, etc. They are usually large plain buildings in industrial areas of cities and towns.
   a. 28-hour day
   b. 1990 Clean Air Act
   c. 33 Strategies of War
   d. Warehouse

33. _____ or Postponement is a concept in supply chain management where the manufacturing process starts by making a generic or family product that is later differentiated into a specific end-product. This is a widely used method, especially in industries with high demand uncertainty, and can be effectively used to address the final demand even if forecasts cannot be improved.

An example would be Benetton and their knitted sweaters that are initially all white, and then dyed into different colors only when the season/customer color preference/demand is known.

   a. Supply-Chain Operations Reference
   b. Materials management
   c. Demand chain
   d. Delayed differentiation

34. _____ is the use of an object (typically referred to as an RFID tag) applied to or incorporated into a product, animal, or person for the purpose of identification and tracking using radio waves. Some tags can be read from several meters away and beyond the line of sight of the reader.

Most RFID tags contain at least two parts.

*Chapter 4. SUPPLY CHAIN MANAGEMENT* 43

   a. 28-hour day
   b. 33 Strategies of War
   c. 1990 Clean Air Act
   d. Radio-frequency identification



35. _____ is a business term which refers to a range of software tools or modules used in executing supply chain transactions, managing supplier relationships and controlling associated business processes.

While functionality in such systems can often be broad - it commonly includes:

   1. Customer requirement processing
   2. Purchase order processing
   3. Inventory management
   4. Goods receipt and Warehouse management
   5. Supplier Management/Sourcing

A requirement of many _____ often includes forecasting. Such tools often attempt to balance the disparity between supply and demand by improving business processes and using algorithms and consumption analysis to better plan future needs. _____ also often includes integration technology that allows organizations to trade electronically with supply chain partners.

   a. Vendor Managed Inventory
   b. Demand chain
   c. Supply-Chain Operations Reference
   d. Supply chain management software



36. _____ is the process whereby an organization establishes the parameters within which programs, investments, and acquisitions are reaching the desired results. Performance Reference Model of the Federal Enterprise Architecture, 2005.

This process of measuring performance often requires the use of statistical evidence to determine progress toward specific defined organizational objectives.

There are many types of measurements.

   a. Crisis management
   b. CIFMS
   c. Workflow
   d. Performance measurement

## Chapter 4. SUPPLY CHAIN MANAGEMENT

37. The _____ is a concept from business management that was first described and popularized by Michael Porter in his 1985 best-seller, Competitive Advantage: Creating and Sustaining Superior Performance.

A _____ is a chain of activities. Products pass through all activities of the chain in order and at each activity the product gains some value. The chain of activities gives the products more added value than the sum of added values of all activities. It is important not to mix the concept of the _____ with the costs occurring throughout the activities.

   a. Value chain
   b. Market development
   c. Customer relationship management
   d. Mass marketing

## Chapter 5. TOTAL QUALITY MANAGEMENT

1. _____ is a business management strategy aimed at embedding awareness of quality in all organizational processes. _____ has been widely used in manufacturing, education, hospitals, call centers, government, and service industries, as well as NASA space and science programs.

As defined by the International Organization for Standardization (ISO):

' _____ is a management approach for an organization, centered on quality, based on the participation of all its members and aiming at long-term success through customer satisfaction, and benefits to all members of the organization and to society.' ISO 8402:1994

One major aim is to reduce variation from every process so that greater consistency of effort is obtained. (Royse, D., Thyer, B., Padgett D., ' Logan T., 2006)

   a. Quality management
   b. 1990 Clean Air Act
   c. 28-hour day
   d. Total quality management


2. _____ can be considered to have three main components: quality control, quality assurance and quality improvement. _____ is focused not only on product quality, but also the means to achieve it. _____ therefore uses quality assurance and control of processes as well as products to achieve more consistent quality.
   a. Total quality management
   b. 28-hour day
   c. Quality management
   d. 1990 Clean Air Act


3. _____ is an advertisement in which a particular product specifically mentions a competitor by name for the express purpose of showing why the competitor is inferior to the product naming it.

This should not be confused with parody advertisements, where a fictional product is being advertised for the purpose of poking fun at the particular advertisement, nor should it be confused with the use of a coined brand name for the purpose of comparing the product without actually naming an actual competitor. ('Wikipedia tastes better and is less filling than the Encyclopedia Galactica.')

In the 1980s, during what has been referred to as the cola wars, soft-drink manufacturer Pepsi ran a series of advertisements where people, caught on hidden camera, in a blind taste test, chose Pepsi over rival Coca-Cola.

## Chapter 5. TOTAL QUALITY MANAGEMENT

a. 1990 Clean Air Act
b. 33 Strategies of War
c. Comparative advertising
d. 28-hour day


4. In economics, business, retail, and accounting, a _____ is the value of money that has been used up to produce something, and hence is not available for use anymore. In economics, a _____ is an alternative that is given up as a result of a decision. In business, the _____ may be one of acquisition, in which case the amount of money expended to acquire it is counted as _____.

 a. Cost overrun
 b. Fixed costs
 c. Cost
 d. Cost allocation


5. The concept of quality costs is a means to quantify the total _____-related efforts and deficiencies. It was first described by Armand V. Feigenbaum in a 1956 Harvard Business Review article.

Prior to its introduction, the general perception was that higher quality requires higher costs, either by buying better materials or machines or by hiring more labor.

 a. Fixed costs
 b. Quality costs
 c. Cost of quality
 d. Cost accounting


6. _____ is a technical term used in management science popularized by Joseph M. Juran

He defined an internal and external customers as anyone affected by the product or by the process used to produce the product, in the context of quality management. _____s may play the role as supplier, processer, and customer in the sequence of product development.

He claimed that the organization must understand and identify both internal and external customers and their needs.

 a. A4e
 b. AAAI
 c. A Stake in the Outcome
 d. Internal customer

## Chapter 5. TOTAL QUALITY MANAGEMENT

7. _____ is one of the managerial functions like planning, organizing, staffing and directing. It is an important function because it helps to check the errors and to take the corrective action so that deviation from standards are minimized and stated goals of the organization are achieved in desired manner. According to modern concepts, _____ is a foreseeing action whereas earlier concept of _____ was used only when errors were detected. _____ in management means setting standards, measuring actual performance and taking corrective action.
   a. Turnover
   b. Schedule of reinforcement
   c. Decision tree pruning
   d. Control

8. In probability theory, a probability distribution is called _____ if its cumulative distribution function is _____. This is equivalent to saying that for random variables X with the distribution in question, Pr[X = a] = 0 for all real numbers a, i.e.: the probability that X attains the value a is zero, for any number a. If the distribution of X is _____ then X is called a _____ random variable.
   a. Continuous
   b. Pay Band
   c. Decision tree pruning
   d. Connectionist expert systems

9. _____ is a management process whereby delivery (customer valued) processes are constantly evaluated and improved in the light of their efficiency, effectiveness and flexibility.

Some see it as a meta process for most management systems (Business Process Management, Quality Management, Project Management). Deming saw it as part of the 'system' whereby feedback from the process and customer were evaluated against organisational goals.

   a. Continuous Improvement Process
   b. Sole proprietorship
   c. First-mover advantage
   d. Critical Success Factor

10. _____ is a Japanese philosophy that focuses on continuous improvement throughout all aspects of life. When applied to the workplace, _____ activities continually improve all functions of a business, from manufacturing to management and from the CEO to the assembly line workers. By improving standardized activities and processes, _____ aims to eliminate waste.

a. Cross-docking
b. Kaizen
c. Psychological pricing
d. Sensitivity analysis

11. The _____ is a graphical depiction of loss developed by the Japanese business statistician Genichi Taguchi to describe a phenomenon affecting the value of products produced by a company. Praised by Dr. W. Edwards Deming, it made clear the concept that quality does not suddenly plummet when, for instance, a machinist exceeds a rigid blueprint tolerance. Instead 'loss' in value progressively increases as variation increases from the intended condition. This was considered a breakthrough in describing quality, and helped fuel the continuous improvement movement that since has become known as lean manufacturing.
a. 33 Strategies of War
b. 1990 Clean Air Act
c. 28-hour day
d. Taguchi loss function

12. In statistics, decision theory and economics, a _____ is a function that maps an event (technically an element of a sample space) onto a real number representing the economic cost or regret associated with the event.

Less technically, in statistics a _____ represents the loss (cost in money or loss in utility in some other sense) associated with an estimate being 'wrong' (different from either a desired or a true value) as a function of a measure of the degree of wrongness (generally the difference between the estimated value and the true or desired value.)

Both Frequentist and Bayesian statistical theory involve calculating statistics in such a way as to minimize the expected loss observed from being wrong given a set of assumptions about the data and one's _____.

a. 1990 Clean Air Act
b. 28-hour day
c. 33 Strategies of War
d. Loss function

13. _____ ('Plan-Do-Check-Act') is an iterative four-step problem-solving process typically used in business process improvement. It is also known as the Deming Cycle, Shewhart cycle, Deming Wheel, or Plan-Do-Study-Act.

_____ was made popular by Dr. W. Edwards Deming, who is considered by many to be the father of modern quality control; however it was always referred to by him as the Shewhart cycle. Later in Deming's career, he modified _____ to Plan, Do, Study, Act (PDSA) so as to better describe his recommendations.

a. Decentralization
b. Management by exception
c. Management team
d. PDCA

14. _____ is the process of comparing the cost, cycle time, productivity, or quality of a specific process or method to another that is widely considered to be an industry standard or best practice. Essentially, _____ provides a snapshot of the performance of your business and helps you understand where you are in relation to a particular standard. The result is often a business case for making changes in order to make improvements.
   a. Competitive heterogeneity
   b. Cost leadership
   c. Complementors
   d. Benchmarking

15. _____ refers to increasing the spiritual, political, social or economic strength of individuals and communities. It often involves the empowered developing confidence in their own capacities.

The term Human _____ covers a vast landscape of meanings, interpretations, definitions and disciplines ranging from psychology and philosophy to the highly commercialized Self-Help industry and Motivational sciences.

   a. AAAI
   b. A Stake in the Outcome
   c. A4e
   d. Empowerment

16. A _____ is a volunteer group composed of workers (or even students), usually under the leadership of their supervisor (but they can elect a team leader), who are trained to identify, analyse and solve work-related problems and present their solutions to management in order to improve the performance of the organization, and motivate and enrich the work of employees. When matured, true _____s become self-managing, having gained the confidence of management.
   _____s are an alternative to the dehumanising concept of the Division of Labour, where workers or individuals are treated like robots.
   a. Quality circle
   b. Certified in Production and Inventory Management
   c. Competency-based job descriptions
   d. Connectionist expert systems

## Chapter 5. TOTAL QUALITY MANAGEMENT

17.  A _____ is a common type of chart, that represents an algorithm or process, showing the steps as boxes of various kinds, and their order by connecting these with arrows. _____s are used in analyzing, designing, documenting or managing a process or program in various fields.

The first structured method for documenting process flow, the 'flow process chart', was introduced by Frank Gilbreth to members of ASME in 1921 as the presentation 'Process Charts--First Steps in Finding the One Best Way'.

 a. 28-hour day
 b. 1990 Clean Air Act
 c. 33 Strategies of War
 d. Flowchart


18.  A scatter plot is a type of display using Cartesian coordinates to display values for two variables for a set of data.

The data is displayed as a collection of points, each having the value of one variable determining the position on the horizontal axis and the value of the other variable determining the position on the vertical axis. A scatter plot is also called a scatter chart, _____ and scatter graph.

 a. 1990 Clean Air Act
 b. 28-hour day
 c. 33 Strategies of War
 d. Scatter diagram


19.  The _____ in statistical process control is a tool used to determine whether a manufacturing or business process is in a state of statistical control or not.

If the chart indicates that the process is currently under control then it can be used with confidence to predict the future performance of the process. If the chart indicates that the process being monitored is not in control, the pattern it reveals can help determine the source of variation to be eliminated to bring the process back into control.

 a. Failure rate
 b. Simple moving average
 c. Control chart
 d. Time series analysis

## Chapter 5. TOTAL QUALITY MANAGEMENT

20. In statistics, a _____ is a graphical display of tabulated frequencies, shown as bars. It shows what proportion of cases fall into each of several categories: it is a form of data binning. The categories are usually specified as non-overlapping intervals of some variable.
   a. Standard deviation
   b. Correlation
   c. Statistics
   d. Histogram

21. _____ is a statistical technique in decision making that is used for selection of a limited number of tasks that produce significant overall effect. It uses the Pareto principle - the idea that by doing 20% of work you can generate 80% of the advantage of doing the entire job. Or in terms of quality improvement, a large majority of problems (80%) are produced by a few key causes (20%.)
   a. Pareto analysis
   b. Probability matching
   c. Polychoric correlation
   d. Goodness of fit

22. _____ is a 'method to transform user demands into design quality, to deploy the functions forming quality, and to deploy methods for achieving the design quality into subsystems and component parts, and ultimately to specific elements of the manufacturing process.' , as described by Dr. Yoji Akao, who originally developed _____ in Japan in 1966, when the author combined his work in quality assurance and quality control points with function deployment used in Value Engineering.

   _____ is designed to help planners focus on characteristics of a new or existing product or service from the viewpoints of market segments, company, or technology-development needs. The technique yields graphs and matrices.

   a. 1990 Clean Air Act
   b. Quality function deployment
   c. Learning organization
   d. Hoshin Kanri

23. _____ can be defined as the idea generation, concept development, testing and manufacturing or implementation of a physical object or service. _____ers conceptualize and evaluate ideas, making them tangible through products in a more systematic approach. The role of a _____er encompasses many characteristics of the marketing manager, product manager, industrial designer and design engineer.

## Chapter 5. TOTAL QUALITY MANAGEMENT

a. Abraham Harold Maslow
b. Adam Smith
c. Affiliation
d. Product design

24. _____ is an integrated communications-based process through which individuals and communities discover that existing and newly-identified needs and wants may be satisfied by the products and services of others.

_____ is defined by the American _____ Association as the activity, set of institutions, and processes for creating, communicating, delivering, and exchanging offerings that have value for customers, clients, partners, and society at large. The term developed from the original meaning which referred literally to going to market, as in shopping, or going to a market to buy or sell goods or services.

a. Market development
b. Disruptive technology
c. Customer relationship management
d. Marketing

25. _____ is an operational activity which does an aggregate plan for the production process, in advance of 2 to 18 months, to give an idea to management as to what quantity of materials and other resources are to be procured and when, so that the total cost of operations of the organization is kept to the minimum over that period.

The quantity of outsourcing, subcontracting of items, overtime of labor, numbers to be hired and fired in each period and the amount of inventory to be held in stock and to be backlogged for each period are decided. All of these activities are done within the framework of the company ethics, policies, and long term commitment to the society, community and the country of operation.

a. Earned Schedule
b. Aggregate planning
c. A Stake in the Outcome
d. Earned value management

26. _____ is an inventory strategy that strives to improve the return on investment of a business by reducing in-process inventory and its associated carrying costs. To meet _____ objectives, the process relies on signals between different points in the process. This means the process is often driven by a series of signals, or Kanban, which tell production when to make the next part. Kanban are usually 'tickets' but can be simple visual signals, such as the presence or absence of a part on a shelf. Implemented correctly, _____ can dramatically improve a manufacturing organization's return on investment, quality, and efficiency.

a. 1990 Clean Air Act
b. 33 Strategies of War
c. 28-hour day
d. Just-in-time


27. _____ is an increasingly broadening term with which an organization, or other human system describes the combination of traditionally administrative personnel functions with acquisition and application of skills, knowledge and experience, Employee Relations and resource planning at various levels. The field draws upon concepts developed in Industrial/Organizational Psychology and System Theory. _____ has at least two related interpretations depending on context. The original usage derives from political economy and economics, where it was traditionally called labor, one of four factors of production although this perspective is changing as a function of new and ongoing research into more strategic approaches at national levels. This first usage is used more in terms of '_____ development', and can go beyond just organizations to the level of nations . The more traditional usage within corporations and businesses refers to the individuals within a firm or agency, and to the portion of the organization that deals with hiring, firing, training, and other personnel issues, typically referred to as `_____ management'.
   a. Human resource management
   b. Bradford Factor
   c. Progressive discipline
   d. Human resources


28. A _____ is the system of organizations, people, technology, activities, information and resources involved in moving a product or service from supplier to customer. _____ activities transform natural resources, raw materials and components into a finished product that is delivered to the end customer. In sophisticated _____ systems, used products may re-enter the _____ at any point where residual value is recyclable.
   a. Packaging
   b. Drop shipping
   c. Wholesalers
   d. Supply chain


29. _____ is the management of a network of interconnected businesses involved in the ultimate provision of product and service packages required by end customers (Harland, 1996.) _____ spans all movement and storage of raw materials, work-in-process inventory, and finished goods from point of origin to point of consumption (supply chain.)

The definition an American professional association put forward is that _____ encompasses the planning and management of all activities involved in sourcing, procurement, conversion, and logistics management activities.

a. Freight forwarder
b. Packaging
c. Supply chain management
d. Drop shipping

## Chapter 6. STATISTICAL QUALITY CONTROL

1. The _____ in statistical process control is a tool used to determine whether a manufacturing or business process is in a state of statistical control or not.

If the chart indicates that the process is currently under control then it can be used with confidence to predict the future performance of the process. If the chart indicates that the process being monitored is not in control, the pattern it reveals can help determine the source of variation to be eliminated to bring the process back into control.

   a. Failure rate
   b. Control chart
   c. Time series analysis
   d. Simple moving average

2. _____ are used to describe the main features of a collection of data in quantitative terms. _____ are distinguished from inductive statistics in that they aim to quantitatively summarize a data set, rather than being used to support statements about the population that the data are thought to represent. Even when a data analysis draws its main conclusions using inductive statistical analysis, _____ are generally presented along with more formal analyses, to give the audience an overall sense of the data being analyzed.
   a. Statistics
   b. Failure rate
   c. Statistical inference
   d. Descriptive statistics

3. _____ is an effective method of monitoring a process through the use of control charts. Control charts enable the use of objective criteria for distinguishing background variation from events of significance based on statistical techniques. Much of its power lies in the ability to monitor both process center and its variation about that center.
   a. Single Minute Exchange of Die
   b. Process capability
   c. Quality control
   d. Statistical process control

4. _____ is one of the managerial functions like planning, organizing, staffing and directing. It is an important function because it helps to check the errors and to take the corrective action so that deviation from standards are minimized and stated goals of the organization are achieved in desired manner. According to modern concepts, _____ is a foreseeing action whereas earlier concept of _____ was used only when errors were detected. _____ in management means setting standards, measuring actual performance and taking corrective action.

a. Decision tree pruning
b. Control
c. Turnover
d. Schedule of reinforcement

5. In engineering and manufacturing, _____ and quality engineering are used in developing systems to ensure products or services are designed and produced to meet or exceed customer requirements. Refer to the definition by Merriam-Webster for further information . These systems are often developed in conjunction with other business and engineering disciplines using a cross-functional approach.
   a. Statistical process control
   b. Single Minute Exchange of Die
   c. Quality control
   d. Process capability

6. _____ is a mathematical science pertaining to the collection, analysis, interpretation or explanation, and presentation of data. It also provides tools for prediction and forecasting based on data. It is applicable to a wide variety of academic disciplines, from the natural and social sciences to the humanities, government and business.
   a. Location parameter
   b. Failure rate
   c. Statistics
   d. Simple moving average

7. _____ is a business management strategy, initially implemented by Motorola, that today enjoys widespread application in many sectors of industry.

_____ seeks to improve the quality of process outputs by identifying and removing the causes of defects (errors) and variation in manufacturing and business processes. It uses a set of quality management methods, including statistical methods, and creates a special infrastructure of people within the organization ('Black Belts' etc.)

   a. Six Sigma
   b. Theory of constraints
   c. Takt time
   d. Production line

## Chapter 6. STATISTICAL QUALITY CONTROL

8. In statistics, _____ is:

   - the arithmetic _____
   - the expected value of a random variable, which is also called the population _____.

It is sometimes stated that the '_____' _____s average. This is incorrect if '_____' is taken in the specific sense of 'arithmetic _____' as there are different types of averages: the _____, median, and mode. Other simple statistical analyses use measures of spread, such as range, interquartile range, or standard deviation. For a real-valued random variable X, the _____ is the expectation of X. Note that not every probability distribution has a defined _____; see the Cauchy distribution for an example.

   a. Mean
   b. Control chart
   c. Statistical inference
   d. Correlation


9. _____ is one of the four elements of marketing mix. An organization or set of organizations (go-betweens) involved in the process of making a product or service available for use or consumption by a consumer or business user.

The other three parts of the marketing mix are product, pricing, and promotion.

   a. Matching theory
   b. Job creation programs
   c. Missing completely at random
   d. Distribution


10. In probability theory and statistics, _____ is a measure of the variability or dispersion of a population, a data set, or a probability distribution. A low _____ indicates that the data points tend to be very close to the same value (the mean), while high _____ indicates that the data are 'spread out' over a large range of values.

For example, the average height for adult men in the United States is about 70 inches (178 cm), with a _____ of around 3 in (8 cm.)

   a. Frequency distribution
   b. Normal distribution
   c. Standard deviation
   d. Failure rate

11. The _____ is a measurable property of a process to the specification, expressed as a _____ index (e.g., $C_{pk}$ or $C_{pm}$) or as a process performance index (e.g., $P_{pk}$ or $P_{pm}$.) The output of this measurement is usually illustrated by a histogram and calculations that predict how many parts will be produced out of specification.

_____ is also defined as the capability of a process to meet its purpose as managed by an organization's management and process definition structures ISO 15504.

   a. Single Minute Exchange of Die
   b. Quality control
   c. Statistical process control
   d. Process capability


12. Engineering _____ is the permissible limit of variation in

   1. a physical dimension,
   2. a measured value or physical property of a material, manufactured object, system, or service,
   3. other measured values (such as temperature, humidity, etc.)
   4. in engineering and safety, a physical distance or space (_____), as in a truck (lorry), train or boat under a bridge as well as a train in a tunnel

Dimensions, properties, or conditions may vary within certain practical limits without significantly affecting functioning of equipment or a process. _____s are specified to allow reasonable leeway for imperfections and inherent variability without compromising performance.

The _____ may be specified as a factor or percentage of the nominal value, a maximum deviation from a nominal value, an explicit range of allowed values, be specified by a note or published standard with this information, or be implied by the numeric accuracy of the nominal value. _____ can be symmetrical, as in 40±0.1, or asymmetrical, such as 40+0.2/−0.1.

   a. Root cause analysis
   b. Zero defects
   c. Quality assurance
   d. Tolerance

## Chapter 6. STATISTICAL QUALITY CONTROL

13. In quality assessment, _____ is an inspection standard describing the maximum number of defects that could be considered acceptable during the random sampling of an inspection. The defects found during inspection are classified into three levels: critical, major and minor. Broadly, these levels are defined as follows:

- Critical defects are those that render the product unsafe or hazardous for the end user, or that contravene mandatory regulations.

- Major defects can result in the product's failure, reducing its marketability, usability, or saleability.

- Minor defects do not affect the product's marketability or usability, but represent workmanship defects that make the product fall short of defined quality standards.

Different companies maintain different interpretations of each defect type.

a. A4e
b. AAAI
c. A Stake in the Outcome
d. Acceptable quality level


14. In decision theory and estimation theory, the _____ of an estimator, $\hat{\theta}$, of an unknown parameter of the distribution, θ, is the expected value of the loss function

$$R(\theta, \hat{\theta}) = \mathbb{E}_\theta L(\theta, \hat{\theta}) = \int L(\theta, \hat{\theta}) \, dP_\theta.$$

## Chapter 6. STATISTICAL QUALITY CONTROL

where $dP_\theta$ is a probability measure parametrized by θ.

- For a scalar parameter θ and a quadratic loss function,

$$L(\theta, \hat{\theta}) = (\theta - \hat{\theta})^2$$

the _____ function becomes the mean squared error of the estimate,

$$R(\theta, \hat{\theta}) = E_\theta (\theta - \hat{\theta})^2$$

- In density estimation, the unknown parameter is probability density itself. The loss function is typically chosen to be a norm in an appropriate function space. For example, for $L^2$ norm,

$$L(f, \hat{f}) = \|f - \hat{f}\|_2^2$$

the _____ function becomes the mean integrated squared error

$$R(f, \hat{f}) = E\|f - \hat{f}\|^2$$

    a. Financial modeling
    b. Risk aversion
    c. Linear model
    d. Risk

15. _____ typically deals with the probability of several successive decisions, each of which has two possible outcomes.

The probability of an event can be expressed as a _____ if its outcomes can be broken down into two probabilities p and q, where p and q are complementary (i.e. p + q = 1) For example, tossing a coin can be either heads or tails, each which have a (theoretical) probability of 0.5. Rolling a four on a six-sided die can be expressed as the probability (1/6) of getting a 4 or the probability (5/6) of rolling something else.

    a. Factorial moment generating function
    b. Binomial probability
    c. Graphical model
    d. Sample space

16. _____ is a way of expressing knowledge or belief that an event will occur or has occurred. In mathematics the concept has been given an exact meaning in _____ theory, that is used extensively in such areas of study as mathematics, statistics, finance, gambling, science, and philosophy to draw conclusions about the likelihood of potential events and the underlying mechanics of complex systems.

The word _____ does not have a consistent direct definition.

   a. Time series analysis
   b. Statistics
   c. Standard deviation
   d. Probability


17. _____ consists of the mental process of thinking involved with the process of judging the merits of multiple options and selecting one of them for action. Some simple examples include deciding whether to get up in the morning or go back to sleep, or selecting a given route for a journey. More complex examples (often decisions that affect what a person thinks or their core beliefs) include choosing a lifestyle, religious affiliation, or political position.
   a. Trade study
   b. Choice
   c. Groups decision making
   d. Championship mobilization


18. In economics, business, retail, and accounting, a _____ is the value of money that has been used up to produce something, and hence is not available for use anymore. In economics, a _____ is an alternative that is given up as a result of a decision. In business, the _____ may be one of acquisition, in which case the amount of money expended to acquire it is counted as _____.
   a. Fixed costs
   b. Cost overrun
   c. Cost allocation
   d. Cost


19. _____ is an advertisement in which a particular product specifically mentions a competitor by name for the express purpose of showing why the competitor is inferior to the product naming it.

This should not be confused with parody advertisements, where a fictional product is being advertised for the purpose of poking fun at the particular advertisement, nor should it be confused with the use of a coined brand name for the purpose of comparing the product without actually naming an actual competitor. ('Wikipedia tastes better and is less filling than the Encyclopedia Galactica.')

In the 1980s, during what has been referred to as the cola wars, soft-drink manufacturer Pepsi ran a series of advertisements where people, caught on hidden camera, in a blind taste test, chose Pepsi over rival Coca-Cola.

a. 28-hour day
b. 33 Strategies of War
c. 1990 Clean Air Act
d. Comparative advertising

20. _____ is an increasingly broadening term with which an organization, or other human system describes the combination of traditionally administrative personnel functions with acquisition and application of skills, knowledge and experience, Employee Relations and resource planning at various levels. The field draws upon concepts developed in Industrial/Organizational Psychology and System Theory. _____ has at least two related interpretations depending on context. The original usage derives from political economy and economics, where it was traditionally called labor, one of four factors of production although this perspective is changing as a function of new and ongoing research into more strategic approaches at national levels. This first usage is used more in terms of '_____ development', and can go beyond just organizations to the level of nations . The more traditional usage within corporations and businesses refers to the individuals within a firm or agency, and to the portion of the organization that deals with hiring, firing, training, and other personnel issues, typically referred to as `_____ management'.
a. Progressive discipline
b. Bradford Factor
c. Human resource management
d. Human resources

21. _____ is an integrated communications-based process through which individuals and communities discover that existing and newly-identified needs and wants may be satisfied by the products and services of others.

_____ is defined by the American _____ Association as the activity, set of institutions, and processes for creating, communicating, delivering, and exchanging offerings that have value for customers, clients, partners, and society at large. The term developed from the original meaning which referred literally to going to market, as in shopping, or going to a market to buy or sell goods or services.

a. Disruptive technology
b. Market development
c. Customer relationship management
d. Marketing

22. _____ is an operational activity which does an aggregate plan for the production process, in advance of 2 to 18 months, to give an idea to management as to what quantity of materials and other resources are to be procured and when, so that the total cost of operations of the organization is kept to the minimum over that period.

The quantity of outsourcing, subcontracting of items, overtime of labor, numbers to be hired and fired in each period and the amount of inventory to be held in stock and to be backlogged for each period are decided. All of these activities are done within the framework of the company ethics, policies, and long term commitment to the society, community and the country of operation.

a. Earned value management
b. A Stake in the Outcome
c. Earned Schedule
d. Aggregate planning


23. A _____ is the system of organizations, people, technology, activities, information and resources involved in moving a product or service from supplier to customer. _____ activities transform natural resources, raw materials and components into a finished product that is delivered to the end customer. In sophisticated _____ systems, used products may re-enter the _____ at any point where residual value is recyclable.
a. Wholesalers
b. Packaging
c. Drop shipping
d. Supply chain


24. _____ is the management of a network of interconnected businesses involved in the ultimate provision of product and service packages required by end customers (Harland, 1996.) _____ spans all movement and storage of raw materials, work-in-process inventory, and finished goods from point of origin to point of consumption (supply chain.)

The definition an American professional association put forward is that _____ encompasses the planning and management of all activities involved in sourcing, procurement, conversion, and logistics management activities.

a. Drop shipping
b. Packaging
c. Freight forwarder
d. Supply chain management

## Chapter 7. JUST-IN-TIME AND LEAN SYSTEMS

1. _____ is an inventory strategy that strives to improve the return on investment of a business by reducing in-process inventory and its associated carrying costs. To meet _____ objectives, the process relies on signals between different points in the process. This means the process is often driven by a series of signals, or Kanban, which tell production when to make the next part. Kanban are usually 'tickets' but can be simple visual signals, such as the presence or absence of a part on a shelf. Implemented correctly, _____ can dramatically improve a manufacturing organization's return on investment, quality, and efficiency.
   a. 28-hour day
   b. 33 Strategies of War
   c. 1990 Clean Air Act
   d. Just-in-time

2. _____ is a Japanese philosophy that focuses on continuous improvement throughout all aspects of life. When applied to the workplace, _____ activities continually improve all functions of a business, from manufacturing to management and from the CEO to the assembly line workers. By improving standardized activities and processes, _____ aims to eliminate waste.
   a. Cross-docking
   b. Psychological pricing
   c. Sensitivity analysis
   d. Kaizen

3. In probability theory, a probability distribution is called _____ if its cumulative distribution function is _____. This is equivalent to saying that for random variables X with the distribution in question, Pr[X = a] = 0 for all real numbers a, i.e.: the probability that X attains the value a is zero, for any number a. If the distribution of X is _____ then X is called a _____ random variable.
   a. Pay Band
   b. Connectionist expert systems
   c. Decision tree pruning
   d. Continuous

4. _____ is a management process whereby delivery (customer valued) processes are constantly evaluated and improved in the light of their efficiency, effectiveness and flexibility.

Some see it as a meta process for most management systems (Business Process Management, Quality Management, Project Management). Deming saw it as part of the 'system' whereby feedback from the process and customer were evaluated against organisational goals.

## Chapter 7. JUST-IN-TIME AND LEAN SYSTEMS

a. Continuous Improvement Process
b. Sole proprietorship
c. First-mover advantage
d. Critical Success Factor


5. _____ is a concept related to lean and just-in-time (JIT) production. The Japanese word _____ is a common term meaning 'signboard' or 'billboard'. According to Taiichi Ohno, the man credited with developing JIT, _____ is a means through which JIT is achieved.
   a. Succession planning
   b. Risk management
   c. Kanban
   d. Trademark


6. A _____ is a plan for production, staffing, inventory, etc. It is usually linked to manufacturing where the plan indicates when and how much of each product will be demanded. This plan quantifies significant processes, parts, and other resources in order to optimize production, to identify bottlenecks, and to anticipate needs and completed goods.
   a. Value engineering
   b. Master production schedule
   c. Remanufacturing
   d. Piecework


7. _____ refers to the difference between the cost of materials purchased by a company plus the cost of the labor to assemble a product and the price at which the company sells the product. An example is the price of gasoline at the pump over the price of the oil in it. In national accounts used in macroeconomics, it refers to the contribution of the factors of production, i.e., land, labor, and capital goods, to raising the value of a product and corresponds to the incomes received by the owners of these factors.
   a. Value added
   b. Deregulation
   c. Rehn-Meidner Model
   d. Minimum wage


8. In economics, business, retail, and accounting, a _____ is the value of money that has been used up to produce something, and hence is not available for use anymore. In economics, a _____ is an alternative that is given up as a result of a decision. In business, the _____ may be one of acquisition, in which case the amount of money expended to acquire it is counted as _____.

a. Cost allocation
b. Cost
c. Cost overrun
d. Fixed costs


9. In quality assessment, _____ is an inspection standard describing the maximum number of defects that could be considered acceptable during the random sampling of an inspection. The defects found during inspection are classified into three levels: critical, major and minor. Broadly, these levels are defined as follows:

- Critical defects are those that render the product unsafe or hazardous for the end user, or that contravene mandatory regulations.

- Major defects can result in the product's failure, reducing its marketability, usability, or saleability.

- Minor defects do not affect the product's marketability or usability, but represent workmanship defects that make the product fall short of defined quality standards.

Different companies maintain different interpretations of each defect type.

a. A4e
b. AAAI
c. Acceptable quality level
d. A Stake in the Outcome


10. _____ is a business management strategy aimed at embedding awareness of quality in all organizational processes. _____ has been widely used in manufacturing, education, hospitals, call centers, government, and service industries, as well as NASA space and science programs.

As defined by the International Organization for Standardization (ISO):

'_____ is a management approach for an organization, centered on quality, based on the participation of all its members and aiming at long-term success through customer satisfaction, and benefits to all members of the organization and to society.' ISO 8402:1994

One major aim is to reduce variation from every process so that greater consistency of effort is obtained. (Royse, D., Thyer, B., Padgett D., ' Logan T., 2006)

## Chapter 7. JUST-IN-TIME AND LEAN SYSTEMS

a. 28-hour day
b. 1990 Clean Air Act
c. Quality management
d. Total quality management

11. The _____ captures an expanded spectrum of values and criteria for measuring organizational success: economic, ecological and social. With the ratification of the United Nations and ICLEI _____ standard for urban and community accounting in early 2007, this became the dominant approach to public sector full cost accounting. Similar UN standards apply to natural capital and human capital measurement to assist in measurements required by _____, e.g. the ecoBudget standard for reporting ecological footprint.
   a. Triple bottom line
   b. 1990 Clean Air Act
   c. 33 Strategies of War
   d. 28-hour day

12. _____ can be considered to have three main components: quality control, quality assurance and quality improvement. _____ is focused not only on product quality, but also the means to achieve it. _____ therefore uses quality assurance and control of processes as well as products to achieve more consistent quality.
   a. Quality management
   b. 1990 Clean Air Act
   c. Total quality management
   d. 28-hour day

13. Autonomation describes a feature of machine design to effect the principle of _____ used in the Toyota Production System (TPS) and Lean manufacturing. It may be described as 'intelligent automation' or 'automation with a human touch.' This type of automation implements some supervisory functions rather than production functions. At Toyota this usually means that if an abnormal situation arises the machine stops and the worker will stop the production line.
   a. Homeworkers
   b. MRP II
   c. Jidoka
   d. Manufacturing resource planning

14. _____ is used for the design, development, analysis, and optimization of technical processes and is mainly applied to chemical plants and chemical processes, but also to power stations, and similar technical facilities. Process flow diagram of a typical amine treating process used in industrial plants

## Chapter 7. JUST-IN-TIME AND LEAN SYSTEMS

_____ is a model-based representation of chemical, physical, biological, and other technical processes and unit operations in software. Basic prerequisites are a thorough knowledge of chemical and physical properties of pure components and mixtures, of reactions, and of mathematical models which, in combination, allow the calculation of a process in computers.

a. 28-hour day
b. 33 Strategies of War
c. Process simulation
d. 1990 Clean Air Act


15. _____ is an advertisement in which a particular product specifically mentions a competitor by name for the express purpose of showing why the competitor is inferior to the product naming it.

This should not be confused with parody advertisements, where a fictional product is being advertised for the purpose of poking fun at the particular advertisement, nor should it be confused with the use of a coined brand name for the purpose of comparing the product without actually naming an actual competitor. ('Wikipedia tastes better and is less filling than the Encyclopedia Galactica.')

In the 1980s, during what has been referred to as the cola wars, soft-drink manufacturer Pepsi ran a series of advertisements where people, caught on hidden camera, in a blind taste test, chose Pepsi over rival Coca-Cola.

a. 1990 Clean Air Act
b. 33 Strategies of War
c. 28-hour day
d. Comparative advertising


16. _____ can be defined as the idea generation, concept development, testing and manufacturing or implementation of a physical object or service. _____ers conceptualize and evaluate ideas, making them tangible through products in a more systematic approach. The role of a _____er encompasses many characteristics of the marketing manager, product manager, industrial designer and design engineer.
a. Affiliation
b. Abraham Harold Maslow
c. Adam Smith
d. Product design


17. _____ is a Japanese term that means 'fail-safing' or 'mistake-proofing'. A _____ is any mechanism in a Lean manufacturing process that helps an equipment operator avoid (yokeru) mistakes (poka.) Its purpose is to eliminate product defects by preventing, correcting, or drawing attention to human errors as they occur.

## Chapter 7. JUST-IN-TIME AND LEAN SYSTEMS

a. 33 Strategies of War
b. Poka-yoke
c. 1990 Clean Air Act
d. 28-hour day

18. A _____ is a volunteer group composed of workers (or even students), usually under the leadership of their supervisor (but they can elect a team leader), who are trained to identify, analyse and solve work-related problems and present their solutions to management in order to improve the performance of the organization, and motivate and enrich the work of employees. When matured, true _____s become self-managing, having gained the confidence of management. _____s are an alternative to the dehumanising concept of the Division of Labour, where workers or individuals are treated like robots.

a. Certified in Production and Inventory Management
b. Competency-based job descriptions
c. Connectionist expert systems
d. Quality circle

19. _____ is a contract between two parties, one being the employer and the other being the employee. An employee may be defined as: 'A person in the service of another under any contract of hire, express or implied, oral or written, where the employer has the power or right to control and direct the employee in the material details of how the work is to be performed.' Black's Law Dictionary page 471 (5th ed. 1979.)

a. Employment rate
b. Employment counsellor
c. Exit interview
d. Employment

20. The metastability in flip-flops can be avoided by ensuring that the data and control inputs are held valid and constant for specified periods before and after the clock pulse, called the _____ and the hold time ($t_h$) respectively. These times are specified in the data sheet for the device, and are typically between a few nanoseconds and a few hundred picoseconds for modern devices.

Unfortunately, it is not always possible to meet the setup and hold criteria, because the flip-flop may be connected to a real-time signal that could change at any time, outside the control of the designer.

a. 28-hour day
b. 33 Strategies of War
c. Setup time
d. 1990 Clean Air Act

## Chapter 7. JUST-IN-TIME AND LEAN SYSTEMS

21. _____ is an integrated communications-based process through which individuals and communities discover that existing and newly-identified needs and wants may be satisfied by the products and services of others.

_____ is defined by the American _____ Association as the activity, set of institutions, and processes for creating, communicating, delivering, and exchanging offerings that have value for customers, clients, partners, and society at large. The term developed from the original meaning which referred literally to going to market, as in shopping, or going to a market to buy or sell goods or services.

   a. Market development
   b. Marketing
   c. Customer relationship management
   d. Disruptive technology

22. A _____ is the system of organizations, people, technology, activities, information and resources involved in moving a product or service from supplier to customer. _____ activities transform natural resources, raw materials and components into a finished product that is delivered to the end customer. In sophisticated _____ systems, used products may re-enter the _____ at any point where residual value is recyclable.
   a. Packaging
   b. Wholesalers
   c. Drop shipping
   d. Supply chain

23. _____ is the management of a network of interconnected businesses involved in the ultimate provision of product and service packages required by end customers (Harland, 1996.) _____ spans all movement and storage of raw materials, work-in-process inventory, and finished goods from point of origin to point of consumption (supply chain.)

The definition an American professional association put forward is that _____ encompasses the planning and management of all activities involved in sourcing, procurement, conversion, and logistics management activities.

   a. Freight forwarder
   b. Drop shipping
   c. Packaging
   d. Supply chain management

24. _____ is an operational activity which does an aggregate plan for the production process, in advance of 2 to 18 months, to give an idea to management as to what quantity of materials and other resources are to be procured and when, so that the total cost of operations of the organization is kept to the minimum over that period.

The quantity of outsourcing, subcontracting of items, overtime of labor, numbers to be hired and fired in each period and the amount of inventory to be held in stock and to be backlogged for each period are decided. All of these activities are done within the framework of the company ethics, policies, and long term commitment to the society, community and the country of operation.

   a. A Stake in the Outcome
   b. Earned value management
   c. Aggregate planning
   d. Earned Schedule

## Chapter 8. FORECASTING

1. The _____ is a systematic, interactive forecasting method which relies on a panel of independent experts. The carefully selected experts answer questionnaires in two or more rounds. After each round, a facilitator provides an anonymous summary of the experts' forecasts from the previous round as well as the reasons they provided for their judgments.
    a. Quality function deployment
    b. Delphi method
    c. Hoshin Kanri
    d. Learning organization

2. _____ is the process of estimation in unknown situations. Prediction is a similar, but more general term. Both can refer to estimation of time series, cross-sectional or longitudinal data.
    a. 1990 Clean Air Act
    b. 28-hour day
    c. 33 Strategies of War
    d. Forecasting

3. Marketing research is a form of business research and is generally divided into two categories: consumer _____ and business-to-business (B2B) _____, which was previously known as industrial marketing research. Consumer marketing research studies the buying habits of individual people while business-to-business marketing research investigates the markets for products sold by one business to another.

    Consumer _____ is a form of applied sociology that concentrates on understanding the behaviours, whims and preferences, of consumers in a market-based economy, and aims to understand the effects and comparative success of marketing campaigns.

    a. Questionnaire
    b. Mystery shoppers
    c. Questionnaire construction
    d. Market research

4. In statistics, signal processing, and many other fields, a _____ is a sequence of data points, measured typically at successive times, spaced at (often uniform) time intervals. _____ analysis comprises methods that attempt to understand such _____, often either to understand the underlying context of the data points (Where did they come from? What generated them?), or to make forecasts (predictions.) _____ forecasting is the use of a model to forecast future events based on known past events: to forecast future data points before they are measured.
    a. Histogram
    b. Time series
    c. Standard deviation
    d. Moving average

## Chapter 8. FORECASTING

5. In the fields of science, engineering, industry and statistics, _____ is the degree of closeness of a measured or calculated quantity to its actual (true) value. _____ is closely related to precision, also called reproducibility or repeatability, the degree to which further measurements or calculations show the same or similar results. _____ indicates proximity to the true value, precision to the repeatability or reproducibility of the measurement

The results of calculations or a measurement can be accurate but not precise, precise but not accurate, neither, or both.

   a. AAAI
   b. Accuracy
   c. A Stake in the Outcome
   d. A4e


6. _____ of the learning curve effect and the closely related experience curve effect express the relationship between equations for experience and efficiency or between efficiency gains and investment in the effort. The experience of 'learning curves' was first observed by the 19th Century German psychologist Hermann Ebbinghaus according to the difficulty of memorizing varying numbers of verbal stimuli, and subsequent learning about the complex processes of learning are discussed in the

.

The rule used for representing the learning curve effect states that the more times a task has been performed, the less time will be required on each subsequent iteration.

   a. Spatial Decision Support Systems
   b. Models
   c. Point biserial correlation coefficient
   d. Distribution


7. In statistics, many time series exhibit cyclic variation known as _____, periodic variation, or periodic fluctuations. This variation can be either regular or semiregular.

For example, retail sales tend to peak for the Christmas season and then decline after the holidays.

   a. 28-hour day
   b. 1990 Clean Air Act
   c. 33 Strategies of War
   d. Seasonality

## Chapter 8. FORECASTING

8. The term '_____' refers to the concept of collecting information and attempting to spot a pattern in the information. In some fields of study, the term '_____' has more formally-defined meanings.

In project management _____ is a mathematical technique that uses historical results to predict future outcome.

   a. Trend analysis
   b. Least squares
   c. Stepwise regression
   d. Regression analysis

9. In statistics, _____ is:

   - the arithmetic _____
   - the expected value of a random variable, which is also called the population _____.

It is sometimes stated that the '_____' _____s average. This is incorrect if '_____' is taken in the specific sense of 'arithmetic _____' as there are different types of averages: the _____, median, and mode. Other simple statistical analyses use measures of spread, such as range, interquartile range, or standard deviation. For a real-valued random variable X, the _____ is the expectation of X. Note that not every probability distribution has a defined _____; see the Cauchy distribution for an example.

   a. Statistical inference
   b. Control chart
   c. Correlation
   d. Mean

10. A _____ is the unweighted mean of the previous n data points. For example, a 10-day _____ of closing price is the mean of the previous 10 days' closing prices. If those prices are $p_M, p_{M-1}, \ldots, p_{M-9}$ then the formula is

$$SMA = \frac{p_M + p_{M-1} + \cdots + p_{M-9}}{10}$$

When calculating successive values, a new value comes into the sum and an old value drops out, meaning a full summation each time is unnecessary,

$$SMA_{\text{today}} = SMA_{\text{yesterday}} - \frac{p_{M-n}}{n} + \frac{p_M}{n}$$

In technical analysis there are various popular values for n, like 10 days, 40 days, or 200 days.

a. Confidence interval
b. Statistically significant
c. Descriptive statistics
d. Simple moving average

11. In statistics, a _____ rolling mean or running average, is a type of finite impulse response filter used to analyze a set of data points by creating a series of averages of different subsets of the full data set. A _____ is not a single number, but it is a set of numbers, each of which is the average of the corresponding subset of a larger set of data points. A _____ may also use unequal weights for each data value in the subset to emphasize particular values in the subset.
    a. Moving average
    b. Homoscedastic
    c. Standard deviation
    d. Time series analysis

12. In statistics, _____ is a technique that can be applied to time series data, either to produce smoothed data for presentation, or to make forecasts. The time series data themselves are a sequence of observations. The observed phenomenon may be an essentially random process, or it may be an orderly, but noisy, process.
    a. A Stake in the Outcome
    b. AAAI
    c. A4e
    d. Exponential smoothing

13. In statistics and image processing, to smooth a data set is to create an approximating function that attempts to capture important patterns in the data, while leaving out noise or other fine-scale structures/rapid phenomena. Many different algorithms are used in _____. One of the most common algorithms is the 'moving average', often used to try to capture important trends in repeated statistical surveys.
    a. Smoothing
    b. 28-hour day
    c. 33 Strategies of War
    d. 1990 Clean Air Act

14. In statistics, _____ is used for two things:

    - to construct a simple formula that will predict a value or values for a variable given the value of another variable.
    - to test whether and how a given variable is related to another variable or variables.

_____ is a form of regression analysis in which the relationship between one or more independent variables and another variable, called the dependent variable, is modelled by a least squares function, called a _____ equation. This function is a linear combination of one or more model parameters, called regression coefficients. A _____ equation with one independent variable represents a straight line when the predicted value (i.e. the dependent variable from the regression equation) is plotted against the independent variable: this is called a simple _____. However, note that 'linear' does not refer to this straight line, but rather to the way in which the regression coefficients occur in the regression equation.

 a. Clinical decision support systems
 b. Continuous
 c. Strict liability
 d. Linear regression

15. In statistics, _____ indicates the strength and direction of a linear relationship between two random variables. That is in contrast with the usage of the term in colloquial speech, which denotes any relationship, not necessarily linear. In general statistical usage, _____ or co-relation refers to the departure of two random variables from independence.

 a. Correlation
 b. Time series analysis
 c. Heteroskedastic
 d. Median

16. In statistics, a _____ is the difference between the actual or real and the predicted or forecast value of a time series or any other phenomenon of interest.

In simple cases, a forecast is compared with an outcome at a single time-point and a summary of _____s is constructed over a collection of such time-points. Here the forecast may be assessed using the difference or using a proportional error.

 a. 28-hour day
 b. 1990 Clean Air Act
 c. 33 Strategies of War
 d. Forecast error

17. The _____ or simply average deviation of a data set is the average of the absolute deviations and is a summary statistic of statistical dispersion or variability. It is also called the mean absolute deviation, but this is easily confused with the median absolute deviation.

The average absolute deviation of a set $\{x_1, x_2, ..., x_n\}$ is

$\boxed{\times}$ >

The choice of measure of central tendency, m(X), has a marked effect on the value of the average deviation.

  a. AAAI
  b. A Stake in the Outcome
  c. A4e
  d. Average absolute deviation,


18.  In statistics, the _____ of an estimator is one of many ways to quantify the amount by which an estimator differs from the true value of the quantity being estimated. As a loss function, _____ is called squared error loss. _____ measures the average of the square of the 'error.' The error is the amount by which the estimator differs from the quantity to be estimated.
  a. Mean squared error
  b. 1990 Clean Air Act
  c. 28-hour day
  d. 33 Strategies of War


19.  _____ is a concept that aims to enhance supply chain integration by supporting and assisting joint practices. _____ seeks cooperative management of inventory through joint visibility and replenishment of products throughout the supply chain. Information shared between suppliers and retailers aids in planning and satisfying customer demands through a supportive system of shared information.
  a. Groups decision making
  b. Timesheets
  c. Career portfolios
  d. Collaborative Planning, Forecasting and Replenishment

## Chapter 8. FORECASTING

20. _____ is an increasingly broadening term with which an organization, or other human system describes the combination of traditionally administrative personnel functions with acquisition and application of skills, knowledge and experience, Employee Relations and resource planning at various levels. The field draws upon concepts developed in Industrial/Organizational Psychology and System Theory. _____ has at least two related interpretations depending on context. The original usage derives from political economy and economics, where it was traditionally called labor, one of four factors of production although this perspective is changing as a function of new and ongoing research into more strategic approaches at national levels. This first usage is used more in terms of '_____ development', and can go beyond just organizations to the level of nations. The more traditional usage within corporations and businesses refers to the individuals within a firm or agency, and to the portion of the organization that deals with hiring, firing, training, and other personnel issues, typically referred to as `_____ management'.
   a. Progressive discipline
   b. Human resource management
   c. Bradford Factor
   d. Human resources

21. _____ is an integrated communications-based process through which individuals and communities discover that existing and newly-identified needs and wants may be satisfied by the products and services of others.

   _____ is defined by the American _____ Association as the activity, set of institutions, and processes for creating, communicating, delivering, and exchanging offerings that have value for customers, clients, partners, and society at large. The term developed from the original meaning which referred literally to going to market, as in shopping, or going to a market to buy or sell goods or services.

   a. Disruptive technology
   b. Marketing
   c. Customer relationship management
   d. Market development

22. A _____ is the system of organizations, people, technology, activities, information and resources involved in moving a product or service from supplier to customer. _____ activities transform natural resources, raw materials and components into a finished product that is delivered to the end customer. In sophisticated _____ systems, used products may re-enter the _____ at any point where residual value is recyclable.
   a. Drop shipping
   b. Packaging
   c. Wholesalers
   d. Supply chain

23. _____ is the management of a network of interconnected businesses involved in the ultimate provision of product and service packages required by end customers (Harland, 1996.) _____ spans all movement and storage of raw materials, work-in-process inventory, and finished goods from point of origin to point of consumption (supply chain).

## Chapter 8. FORECASTING

The definition an American professional association put forward is that _____ encompasses the planning and management of all activities involved in sourcing, procurement, conversion, and logistics management activities.

a. Freight forwarder
b. Packaging
c. Supply chain management
d. Drop shipping


24. _____ is an operational activity which does an aggregate plan for the production process, in advance of 2 to 18 months, to give an idea to management as to what quantity of materials and other resources are to be procured and when, so that the total cost of operations of the organization is kept to the minimum over that period.

The quantity of outsourcing, subcontracting of items, overtime of labor, numbers to be hired and fired in each period and the amount of inventory to be held in stock and to be backlogged for each period are decided. All of these activities are done within the framework of the company ethics, policies, and long term commitment to the society, community and the country of operation.

a. Earned value management
b. Aggregate planning
c. A Stake in the Outcome
d. Earned Schedule

## Chapter 9. CAPACITY PLANNING AND FACILITY LOCATION

1. _____ is the process of determining the production capacity needed by an organization to meet changing demands for its products. In the context of _____, 'capacity' is the maximum amount of work that an organization is capable of completing in a given period of time.

A discrepancy between the capacity of an organization and the demands of its customers results in inefficiency, either in under-utilized resources or unfulfilled customers.

   a. Scientific management
   b. Productivity
   c. Remanufacturing
   d. Capacity planning


2. _____ is a branch of operations research concerning itself with mathematical modeling and solution of problems concerning the placement of facilities in order to minimize transportation costs, avoid placing hazardous materials near housing, outperform competitors' facilities, etc.

A simple _____ problem is the Fermat-Weber problem, in which a single facility is to be placed, with the only optimization criterion being the minimization of the sum of distances from a given set of point sites. More complex problems considered in this discipline include the placement of multiple facilities, constraints on the locations of facilities, and more complex optimization criteria.

   a. 28-hour day
   b. Facility location
   c. Multiscale decision making
   d. 1990 Clean Air Act


3. In economics and sociology, an _____ is any factor (financial or non-financial) that enables or motivates a particular course of action, or counts as a reason for preferring one choice to the alternatives. It is an expectation that encourages people to behave in a certain way. Since human beings are purposeful creatures, the study of _____ structures is central to the study of all economic activity (both in terms of individual decision-making and in terms of co-operation and competition within a larger institutional structure.)
   a. AAAI
   b. Incentive
   c. A Stake in the Outcome
   d. A4e


4. An _____ is a formal scheme used to promote or encourage specific actions or behavior by a specific group of people during a defined period of time. _____s are particularly used in business management to motivate employees, and in sales in order to attract and retain customers. The scientific literature also refers to this concept as Pay for Performance.

## Chapter 9. CAPACITY PLANNING AND FACILITY LOCATION

a. A Stake in the Outcome
b. AAAI
c. A4e
d. Incentive program

5. _____ is a concept in economics which refers to the extent to which an enterprise or a nation actually uses its installed productive capacity. Thus, it refers to the relationship between actual output that 'is' produced with the installed equipment and the potential output which 'could' be produced with it, if capacity was fully used.

If market demand grows, _____ will rise.

a. Factors of production
b. Capacity utilization
c. Diseconomies of scale
d. Multifactor productivity

6. In queueing theory, _____ is the proportion of the system's resources which is used by the traffic which arrives at it. It should be strictly less than one for the system to function well. It is usually represented by the symbol ρ.

a. A Stake in the Outcome
b. A4e
c. AAAI
d. Utilization

7. _____ are the forces that cause larger firms to produce goods and services at increased per-unit costs. They are less well known than what economists have long understood as 'economies of scale', the forces which enable larger firms to produce goods and services at reduced per-unit costs.

Some of the forces which cause a diseconomy of scale are listed below:

Ideally, all employees of a firm would have one-on-one communication with each other so they know exactly what the other workers are doing.

a. Factors of production
b. Multifactor productivity
c. Production function
d. Diseconomies of scale

## Chapter 9. CAPACITY PLANNING AND FACILITY LOCATION

8. _____, in microeconomics, are the cost advantages that a business obtains due to expansion. They are factors that cause a producer's average cost per unit to fall as scale is increased. _____ is a long run concept and refers to reductions in unit cost as the size of a facility, or scale, increases.
   a. Economies of scope
   b. A Stake in the Outcome
   c. A4e
   d. Economies of scale

9. _____ is an inventory strategy that strives to improve the return on investment of a business by reducing in-process inventory and its associated carrying costs. To meet _____ objectives, the process relies on signals between different points in the process. This means the process is often driven by a series of signals, or Kanban, which tell production when to make the next part. Kanban are usually 'tickets' but can be simple visual signals, such as the presence or absence of a part on a shelf. Implemented correctly, _____ can dramatically improve a manufacturing organization's return on investment, quality, and efficiency.
   a. 1990 Clean Air Act
   b. 33 Strategies of War
   c. 28-hour day
   d. Just-in-time

10. _____ can be regarded as an outcome of mental processes (cognitive process) leading to the selection of a course of action among several alternatives. Every _____ process produces a final choice. The output can be an action or an opinion of choice.
    a. 33 Strategies of War
    b. 28-hour day
    c. 1990 Clean Air Act
    d. Decision making

11. _____ is the process of estimation in unknown situations. Prediction is a similar, but more general term. Both can refer to estimation of time series, cross-sectional or longitudinal data.
    a. 33 Strategies of War
    b. Forecasting
    c. 1990 Clean Air Act
    d. 28-hour day

12. In the fields of science, engineering, industry and statistics, _____ is the degree of closeness of a measured or calculated quantity to its actual (true) value. _____ is closely related to precision, also called reproducibility or repeatability, the degree to which further measurements or calculations show the same or similar results. _____ indicates proximity to the true value, precision to the repeatability or reproducibility of the measurement

## Chapter 9. CAPACITY PLANNING AND FACILITY LOCATION

The results of calculations or a measurement can be accurate but not precise, precise but not accurate, neither, or both.

a. AAAI
b. A Stake in the Outcome
c. A4e
d. Accuracy

13. A _____ is a decision support tool that uses a tree-like graph or model of decisions and their possible consequences, including chance event outcomes, resource costs, and utility. _____ s are commonly used in operations research, specifically in decision analysis, to help identify a strategy most likely to reach a goal. Another use of _____ s is as a descriptive means for calculating conditional probabilities.

a. Decision tree
b. 1990 Clean Air Act
c. 28-hour day
d. 33 Strategies of War

14. In probability theory and statistics, the _____ of a random variable is the integral of the random variable with respect to its probability measure. For discrete random variables this is equivalent to the probability-weighted sum of the possible values, and for continuous random variables with a density function it is the probability density -weighted integral of the possible values.

a. Expected value
b. A Stake in the Outcome
c. A4e
d. AAAI

15. _____ in its literal sense is the process of transformation of local or regional phenomena into global ones. It can be described as a process by which the people of the world are unified into a single society and function together.

This process is a combination of economic, technological, sociocultural and political forces.

a. Cost Management
b. Collaborative Planning, Forecasting and Replenishment
c. Globalization
d. Histogram

## Chapter 9. CAPACITY PLANNING AND FACILITY LOCATION

16. A _____ is a general term that describes any government policy or regulation that restricts international trade. The barriers can take many forms, including the following terms that include many restrictions in international trade within multiple countries that import and export any items of trade.

- Import duty
- Import licenses
- Export licenses
- Import quotas
- Tariffs
- Subsidies
- Non-tariff barriers to trade
- Voluntary Export Restraints
- Local Content Requirements
- Embargo

Most _____s work on the same principle: the imposition of some sort of cost on trade that raises the price of the traded products. If two or more nations repeatedly use _____s against each other, then a trade war results.

a. Most favoured nation
b. Trade creation
c. Customs brokerage
d. Trade barrier


17. In economics, business, retail, and accounting, a _____ is the value of money that has been used up to produce something, and hence is not available for use anymore. In economics, a _____ is an alternative that is given up as a result of a decision. In business, the _____ may be one of acquisition, in which case the amount of money expended to acquire it is counted as _____.

a. Cost overrun
b. Fixed costs
c. Cost allocation
d. Cost


18. _____ of the learning curve effect and the closely related experience curve effect express the relationship between equations for experience and efficiency or between efficiency gains and investment in the effort. The experience of 'learning curves' was first observed by the 19th Century German psychologist Hermann Ebbinghaus according to the difficulty of memorizing varying numbers of verbal stimuli, and subsequent learning about the complex processes of learning are discussed in the

## Chapter 9. CAPACITY PLANNING AND FACILITY LOCATION

The rule used for representing the learning curve effect states that the more times a task has been performed, the less time will be required on each subsequent iteration.

a. Point biserial correlation coefficient
b. Spatial Decision Support Systems
c. Distribution
d. Models

19. _____ is an integrated communications-based process through which individuals and communities discover that existing and newly-identified needs and wants may be satisfied by the products and services of others.

_____ is defined by the American _____ Association as the activity, set of institutions, and processes for creating, communicating, delivering, and exchanging offerings that have value for customers, clients, partners, and society at large. The term developed from the original meaning which referred literally to going to market, as in shopping, or going to a market to buy or sell goods or services.

a. Marketing
b. Market development
c. Customer relationship management
d. Disruptive technology

20. A _____ is a commercial building for storage of goods. _____s are used by manufacturers, importers, exporters, wholesalers, transport businesses, customs, etc. They are usually large plain buildings in industrial areas of cities and towns.
a. Warehouse
b. 33 Strategies of War
c. 1990 Clean Air Act
d. 28-hour day

21. _____ is an operational activity which does an aggregate plan for the production process, in advance of 2 to 18 months, to give an idea to management as to what quantity of materials and other resources are to be procured and when, so that the total cost of operations of the organization is kept to the minimum over that period.

The quantity of outsourcing, subcontracting of items, overtime of labor, numbers to be hired and fired in each period and the amount of inventory to be held in stock and to be backlogged for each period are decided. All of these activities are done within the framework of the company ethics, policies, and long term commitment to the society, community and the country of operation.

a. Earned Schedule
b. A Stake in the Outcome
c. Earned value management
d. Aggregate planning

22. A _____ is the system of organizations, people, technology, activities, information and resources involved in moving a product or service from supplier to customer. _____ activities transform natural resources, raw materials and components into a finished product that is delivered to the end customer. In sophisticated _____ systems, used products may re-enter the _____ at any point where residual value is recyclable.
   a. Drop shipping
   b. Wholesalers
   c. Packaging
   d. Supply chain

23. _____ is the management of a network of interconnected businesses involved in the ultimate provision of product and service packages required by end customers (Harland, 1996.) _____ spans all movement and storage of raw materials, work-in-process inventory, and finished goods from point of origin to point of consumption (supply chain.)

The definition an American professional association put forward is that _____ encompasses the planning and management of all activities involved in sourcing, procurement, conversion, and logistics management activities.

   a. Drop shipping
   b. Packaging
   c. Freight forwarder
   d. Supply chain management

## Chapter 10. FACILITY LAYOUT

1. _____ of the learning curve effect and the closely related experience curve effect express the relationship between equations for experience and efficiency or between efficiency gains and investment in the effort. The experience of 'learning curves' was first observed by the 19th Century German psychologist Hermann Ebbinghaus according to the difficulty of memorizing varying numbers of verbal stimuli, and subsequent learning about the complex processes of learning are discussed in the

.

The rule used for representing the learning curve effect states that the more times a task has been performed, the less time will be required on each subsequent iteration.

   a. Point biserial correlation coefficient
   b. Models
   c. Distribution
   d. Spatial Decision Support Systems

2. A _____ is a commercial building for storage of goods. _____s are used by manufacturers, importers, exporters, wholesalers, transport businesses, customs, etc. They are usually large plain buildings in industrial areas of cities and towns.
   a. Warehouse
   b. 28-hour day
   c. 33 Strategies of War
   d. 1990 Clean Air Act

3. The _____ Method is a tool for scheduling activities in a project plan. It is a method of constructing a project schedule network diagram that uses boxes, referred to as nodes, to represent activities and connects them with arrows that show the dependencies.

   - Critical Tasks, noncritical tasks, and slack time
   - Shows the relationship of the tasks to each other
   - Allows for what-if, worst-case, best-case and most likely scenario

Key elements include determining predecessors and defining attributes such as

   - early start date
   - last-last
   - early finish date
   - late finish date
   - Duration
   - WBS reference

.

a. Precedence diagram
b. Project management office
c. Work package
d. Project manager

4. _____ is an integrated communications-based process through which individuals and communities discover that existing and newly-identified needs and wants may be satisfied by the products and services of others.

_____ is defined by the American _____ Association as the activity, set of institutions, and processes for creating, communicating, delivering, and exchanging offerings that have value for customers, clients, partners, and society at large. The term developed from the original meaning which referred literally to going to market, as in shopping, or going to a market to buy or sell goods or services.

a. Market development
b. Customer relationship management
c. Disruptive technology
d. Marketing

5. _____ is an operational activity which does an aggregate plan for the production process, in advance of 2 to 18 months, to give an idea to management as to what quantity of materials and other resources are to be procured and when, so that the total cost of operations of the organization is kept to the minimum over that period.

The quantity of outsourcing, subcontracting of items, overtime of labor, numbers to be hired and fired in each period and the amount of inventory to be held in stock and to be backlogged for each period are decided. All of these activities are done within the framework of the company ethics, policies, and long term commitment to the society, community and the country of operation.

a. A Stake in the Outcome
b. Aggregate planning
c. Earned value management
d. Earned Schedule

## Chapter 10. FACILITY LAYOUT

6. _____ is an increasingly broadening term with which an organization, or other human system describes the combination of traditionally administrative personnel functions with acquisition and application of skills, knowledge and experience, Employee Relations and resource planning at various levels. The field draws upon concepts developed in Industrial/Organizational Psychology and System Theory. _____ has at least two related interpretations depending on context. The original usage derives from political economy and economics, where it was traditionally called labor, one of four factors of production although this perspective is changing as a function of new and ongoing research into more strategic approaches at national levels. This first usage is used more in terms of '_____ development', and can go beyond just organizations to the level of nations. The more traditional usage within corporations and businesses refers to the individuals within a firm or agency, and to the portion of the organization that deals with hiring, firing, training, and other personnel issues, typically referred to as `_____ management'.
   a. Bradford Factor
   b. Progressive discipline
   c. Human resources
   d. Human resource management


7. A _____ is the system of organizations, people, technology, activities, information and resources involved in moving a product or service from supplier to customer. _____ activities transform natural resources, raw materials and components into a finished product that is delivered to the end customer. In sophisticated _____ systems, used products may re-enter the _____ at any point where residual value is recyclable.
   a. Packaging
   b. Wholesalers
   c. Supply chain
   d. Drop shipping


8. _____ is the management of a network of interconnected businesses involved in the ultimate provision of product and service packages required by end customers (Harland, 1996.) _____ spans all movement and storage of raw materials, work-in-process inventory, and finished goods from point of origin to point of consumption (supply chain.)

The definition an American professional association put forward is that _____ encompasses the planning and management of all activities involved in sourcing, procurement, conversion, and logistics management activities.

   a. Drop shipping
   b. Freight forwarder
   c. Packaging
   d. Supply chain management

## Chapter 11. WORK SYSTEM DESIGN

1. In organizational development (OD), _____ is the application of Socio-Technical Systems principles and techniques to the humanization of work.

The aims of _____ to improved job satisfaction, to improved through-put, to improved quality and to reduced employee problems, e.g., grievances, absenteeism.

Under scientific management people would be directed by reason and the problems of industrial unrest would be appropriately (i.e., scientifically) addressed.

   a. Work design
   b. Graduate recruitment
   c. Path-goal theory
   d. Management process


2. Processes and activities include everything that happens within the _____. The term processes and activities is used instead of the term business process because many _____s do not contain highly structured business processes involving a prescribed sequence of steps, each of which is triggered in a pre-defined manner. Such processes are sometimes described as 'artful processes' whose sequence and content 'depend on the skills, experience, and judgment of the primary actors.' (Hill et al., 2006) In effect, business process is but one of a number of different perspectives for analyzing the activities within a _____.

   a. Split shift
   b. Work system
   c. Work-at-home scheme
   d. Skilled worker


3. The _____ captures an expanded spectrum of values and criteria for measuring organizational success: economic, ecological and social. With the ratification of the United Nations and ICLEI _____ standard for urban and community accounting in early 2007, this became the dominant approach to public sector full cost accounting. Similar UN standards apply to natural capital and human capital measurement to assist in measurements required by _____, e.g. the ecoBudget standard for reporting ecological footprint.
   a. 1990 Clean Air Act
   b. Triple bottom line
   c. 33 Strategies of War
   d. 28-hour day


4. _____ means increasing the scope of a job through extending the range of its job duties and responsibilities. This contradicts the principles of specialisation and the division of labour whereby work is divided into small units, each of which is performed repetitively by an individual worker. Some motivational theories suggest that the boredom and alienation caused by the division of labour can actually cause efficiency to fall.

## Chapter 11. WORK SYSTEM DESIGN

a. Centralization
b. Delayering
c. Mock interview
d. Job enlargement

5. _____ is an attempt to motivate employees by giving them the opportunity to use the range of their abilities. It is an idea that was developed by the American psychologist Frederick Herzberg in the 1950s. It can be contrasted to job enlargement which simply increases the number of tasks without changing the challenge.

a. Cash cow
b. Catfish effect
c. C-A-K-E
d. Job enrichment

6. _____ is an approach to management development where an individual is moved through a schedule of assignments designed to give him or her a breadth of exposure to the entire operation.

_____ is also practiced to allow qualified employees to gain more insights into the processes of a company, and to reduce boredom and increase job satisfaction through job variation.

The term _____ can also mean the scheduled exchange of persons in offices, especially in public offices, prior to the end of incumbency or the legislative period.

a. 1990 Clean Air Act
b. 28-hour day
c. 33 Strategies of War
d. Job rotation

7. _____, e-commuting, e-work, telework, working from home (WFH), or working at home (WAH) is a work arrangement in which employees enjoy flexibility in working location and hours. In other words, the daily commute to a central place of work is replaced by telecommunication links. Many work from home, while others, occasionally also referred to as nomad workers or web commuters utilize mobile telecommunications technology to work from coffee shops or myriad other locations.

a. 28-hour day
b. Telecommuting
c. 33 Strategies of War
d. 1990 Clean Air Act

## Chapter 11. WORK SYSTEM DESIGN

8. _____ is a cross-disciplinary area concerned with protecting the safety, health and welfare of people engaged in work or employment. The goal of all _____ programs is to foster a work free safe environment. As a secondary effect, it may also protect co-workers, family members, employers, customers, suppliers, nearby communities, and other members of the public who are impacted by the workplace environment.

   a. Occupational Safety and Health
   b. AAAI
   c. A4e
   d. A Stake in the Outcome

9. The _____ is the primary federal law which governs occupational health and safety in the private sector and federal government in the United States. It was enacted by Congress in 1970 and was signed by President Richard Nixon on December 29, 1970. Its main goal is to ensure that employers provide employees with an environment free from recognized hazards, such as exposure to toxic chemicals, excessive noise levels, mechanical dangers, heat or cold stress, or unsanitary conditions.

   a. Unemployment and Farm Relief Act
   b. United States Department of Justice
   c. Unemployment Action Center
   d. Occupational Safety and Health Act

10. The United States _____ is an agency of the United States Department of Labor. It was created by Congress under the Occupational Safety and Health Act, signed by President Richard M. Nixon, on December 29, 1970. Its mission is to prevent work-related injuries, illnesses, and deaths by issuing and enforcing rules (called standards) for workplace safety and health.

    a. Unemployment insurance
    b. Opinion leadership
    c. Operant conditioning
    d. Occupational Safety and Health Administration

11. _____ is a business management strategy aimed at embedding awareness of quality in all organizational processes. _____ has been widely used in manufacturing, education, hospitals, call centers, government, and service industries, as well as NASA space and science programs.

As defined by the International Organization for Standardization (ISO):

> '_____ is a management approach for an organization, centered on quality, based on the participation of all its members and aiming at long-term success through customer satisfaction, and benefits to all members of the organization and to society.' ISO 8402:1994

One major aim is to reduce variation from every process so that greater consistency of effort is obtained. (Royse, D., Thyer, B., Padgett D., ' Logan T., 2006)

## Chapter 11. WORK SYSTEM DESIGN

a. Quality management
b. 1990 Clean Air Act
c. 28-hour day
d. Total quality management


12. _____ can be considered to have three main components: quality control, quality assurance and quality improvement. _____ is focused not only on product quality, but also the means to achieve it. _____ therefore uses quality assurance and control of processes as well as products to achieve more consistent quality.

a. 28-hour day
b. 1990 Clean Air Act
c. Quality management
d. Total quality management


13. A time and motion study (or time-motion study) is a business efficiency technique combining the _____ work of Frederick Winslow Taylor with the Motion Study work of Frank and Lillian Gilbreth (not to be confused with their son, best known through the biographical 1950 film and book Cheaper by the Dozen.) It is a major part of scientific management (Taylorism.)

A time and motion study would be used to reduce the number of motions in performing a task in order to increase productivity.

a. 33 Strategies of War
b. Time study
c. 1990 Clean Air Act
d. 28-hour day


14. The _____ system was developed by AMD in the mid-1990s as a method of comparing their x86 processors to those of rival Intel.

The first use of the _____ system was in 1996, when AMD used it to assert that their AMD 5x86 processor was as fast as a Pentium running at 75 MHz. The designation 'P75' was added to the chip to denote this.

a. Performance rating
b. 33 Strategies of War
c. 1990 Clean Air Act
d. 28-hour day

## Chapter 11. WORK SYSTEM DESIGN

15. In economics and sociology, an _____ is any factor (financial or non-financial) that enables or motivates a particular course of action, or counts as a reason for preferring one choice to the alternatives. It is an expectation that encourages people to behave in a certain way. Since human beings are purposeful creatures, the study of _____ structures is central to the study of all economic activity (both in terms of individual decision-making and in terms of co-operation and competition within a larger institutional structure.)

   a. A4e
   b. Incentive
   c. A Stake in the Outcome
   d. AAAI

16. An _____ is a formal scheme used to promote or encourage specific actions or behavior by a specific group of people during a defined period of time. _____s are particularly used in business management to motivate employees, and in sales in order to attract and retain customers. The scientific literature also refers to this concept as Pay for Performance.

   a. A4e
   b. AAAI
   c. A Stake in the Outcome
   d. Incentive program

17. _____, widely known as F. W. Taylor, was an American mechanical engineer who sought to improve industrial efficiency. He is regarded as the father of scientific management, and was one of the first management consultants.

Taylor was one of the intellectual leaders of the Efficiency Movement and his ideas, broadly conceived, were highly influential in the Progressive Era.

   a. Frederick Winslow Taylor
   b. Douglas N. Daft
   c. Geoffrey Colvin
   d. Jonah Jacob Goldberg

18. In economics, collective bargaining, psychology, and political science, 'free riders' are those who consume more than their fair share of a public resource, or shoulder less than a fair share of the costs of its production. Free riding is usually considered to be an economic 'problem' only when it leads to the non-production or under-production of a public good (and thus to Pareto inefficiency), or when it leads to the excessive use of a common property resource. The _____ is the question of how to limit free riding (or its negative effects) in these situations.

a. 28-hour day
b. Free rider problem
c. Natural monopoly
d. 1990 Clean Air Act


19. _____, when used as a special term, refers to various incentive plans introduced by businesses that provide direct or indirect payments to employees that depend on company's profitability in addition to employees' regular salary and bonuses. In publicly traded companies these plans typically amount to allocation of shares to employees.

The _____ plans are based on predetermined economic sharing rules that define the split of gains between the company as a principal and the employee as an agent.

a. Wage
b. Living wage
c. Federal Wage System
d. Profit sharing


20. The term '_____' refers to the concept of collecting information and attempting to spot a pattern in the information. In some fields of study, the term '_____' has more formally-defined meanings.

In project management _____ is a mathematical technique that uses historical results to predict future outcome.

a. Stepwise regression
b. Regression analysis
c. Trend analysis
d. Least squares


21. The term _____ refers to a graphical representation of the 'average' rate of learning for an activity or tool. It can represent at a glance the initial difficulty of learning something and, to an extent, how much there is to learn after initial familiarity. For example, the Windows program Notepad is extremely simple to learn, but offers little after this.
a. Learning curve
b. 1990 Clean Air Act
c. 33 Strategies of War
d. 28-hour day

## Chapter 11. WORK SYSTEM DESIGN

22. _____ is an inventory strategy that strives to improve the return on investment of a business by reducing in-process inventory and its associated carrying costs. To meet _____ objectives, the process relies on signals between different points in the process. This means the process is often driven by a series of signals, or Kanban , which tell production when to make the next part. Kanban are usually 'tickets' but can be simple visual signals, such as the presence or absence of a part on a shelf. Implemented correctly, _____ can dramatically improve a manufacturing organization's return on investment, quality, and efficiency.
   a. 1990 Clean Air Act
   b. 28-hour day
   c. 33 Strategies of War
   d. Just-in-time

23. _____ is an area of business concerned with the production of goods and services, and involves the responsibility of ensuring that business operations are efficient in terms of using as little resource as needed, and effective in terms of meeting customer requirements. It is concerned with managing the process that converts inputs (in the forms of materials, labour and energy) into outputs (in the form of goods and services.)

Operations traditionally refers to the production of goods and services separately, although the distinction between these two main types of operations is increasingly difficult to make as manufacturers tend to merge product and service offerings.

   a. A Stake in the Outcome
   b. AAAI
   c. A4e
   d. Operations management

24. _____ is an increasingly broadening term with which an organization, or other human system describes the combination of traditionally administrative personnel functions with acquisition and application of skills, knowledge and experience, Employee Relations and resource planning at various levels. The field draws upon concepts developed in Industrial/Organizational Psychology and System Theory. _____ has at least two related interpretations depending on context. The original usage derives from political economy and economics, where it was traditionally called labor, one of four factors of production although this perspective is changing as a function of new and ongoing research into more strategic approaches at national levels. This first usage is used more in terms of '_____ development', and can go beyond just organizations to the level of nations . The more traditional usage within corporations and businesses refers to the individuals within a firm or agency, and to the portion of the organization that deals with hiring, firing, training, and other personnel issues, typically referred to as `_____ management'.
   a. Bradford Factor
   b. Human resources
   c. Human resource management
   d. Progressive discipline

## Chapter 11. WORK SYSTEM DESIGN

25. _____ is an integrated communications-based process through which individuals and communities discover that existing and newly-identified needs and wants may be satisfied by the products and services of others.

_____ is defined by the American _____ Association as the activity, set of institutions, and processes for creating, communicating, delivering, and exchanging offerings that have value for customers, clients, partners, and society at large. The term developed from the original meaning which referred literally to going to market, as in shopping, or going to a market to buy or sell goods or services.

   a. Customer relationship management
   b. Disruptive technology
   c. Marketing
   d. Market development


26. _____ is an operational activity which does an aggregate plan for the production process, in advance of 2 to 18 months, to give an idea to management as to what quantity of materials and other resources are to be procured and when, so that the total cost of operations of the organization is kept to the minimum over that period.

The quantity of outsourcing, subcontracting of items, overtime of labor, numbers to be hired and fired in each period and the amount of inventory to be held in stock and to be backlogged for each period are decided. All of these activities are done within the framework of the company ethics, policies, and long term commitment to the society, community and the country of operation.

   a. Earned Schedule
   b. A Stake in the Outcome
   c. Earned value management
   d. Aggregate planning


27. A _____ is the system of organizations, people, technology, activities, information and resources involved in moving a product or service from supplier to customer. _____ activities transform natural resources, raw materials and components into a finished product that is delivered to the end customer. In sophisticated _____ systems, used products may re-enter the _____ at any point where residual value is recyclable.
   a. Packaging
   b. Supply chain
   c. Wholesalers
   d. Drop shipping


28. _____ is the management of a network of interconnected businesses involved in the ultimate provision of product and service packages required by end customers (Harland, 1996.) _____ spans all movement and storage of raw materials, work-in-process inventory, and finished goods from point of origin to point of consumption (supply chain.)

The definition an American professional association put forward is that _____ encompasses the planning and management of all activities involved in sourcing, procurement, conversion, and logistics management activities.

a. Freight forwarder
b. Packaging
c. Drop shipping
d. Supply chain management

## Chapter 12. INDEPENDENT DEMAND INVENTORY MANAGEMENT

1. The '_____ scheme' is an economic term, referring to the use of commodity storage for economic stabilization. Specifically, commodities are bought and stored when there is a surplus in the economy and they are sold from these stores when there are shortages in the economy. The institutional buying, storing and selling of commodities by a large player (e.g. a government) can take place for one commodity or a 'basket of commodities'.
   a. Power
   b. Reservation wage
   c. Buffer stock
   d. Contingent employment

2. _____ is one of the four elements of marketing mix. An organization or set of organizations (go-betweens) involved in the process of making a product or service available for use or consumption by a consumer or business user.

   The other three parts of the marketing mix are product, pricing, and promotion.

   a. Missing completely at random
   b. Job creation programs
   c. Matching theory
   d. Distribution

3. _____ are goods that have completed the manufacturing process but have not yet been sold or distributed to the end user.

   Manufacturing has three classes of inventory:

   1. Raw material
   2. Work in process
   3. _____

   A good purchased as a 'raw material' goes into the manufacture of a product. A good only partially completed during the manufacturing process is called 'work in process'. When the good is completed as to manufacturing but not yet sold or distributed to the end-user is called a 'finished good'.

   a. Finished goods
   b. Reorder point
   c. 28-hour day
   d. 1990 Clean Air Act

4. _____ is a term used by inventory specialists to describe a level of extra stock that is maintained below the cycle stock to buffer against stockouts. _____ exists to counter uncertainties in supply and demand. _____ is defined as extra units of inventory carried as protection against possible stockouts .(shortfall in raw material or packaging.)

## Chapter 12. INDEPENDENT DEMAND INVENTORY MANAGEMENT

a. Process automation
b. Safety stock
c. Knowledge worker
d. Product life cycle

5. A _____ is a commercial building for storage of goods. _____s are used by manufacturers, importers, exporters, wholesalers, transport businesses, customs, etc. They are usually large plain buildings in industrial areas of cities and towns.

a. Warehouse
b. 28-hour day
c. 1990 Clean Air Act
d. 33 Strategies of War

6. _____ is the provision of service to customers before, during and after a purchase.

According to Turban et al. (2002), '_____ is a series of activities designed to enhance the level of customer satisfaction - that is, the feeling that a product or service has met the customer expectation.'

Its importance varies by product, industry and customer; defective or broken merchandise can be exchanged, often only with a receipt and within a specified time frame.

a. Service rate
b. 28-hour day
c. Customer service
d. 1990 Clean Air Act

7. _____ is an advertisement in which a particular product specifically mentions a competitor by name for the express purpose of showing why the competitor is inferior to the product naming it.

This should not be confused with parody advertisements, where a fictional product is being advertised for the purpose of poking fun at the particular advertisement, nor should it be confused with the use of a coined brand name for the purpose of comparing the product without actually naming an actual competitor. ('Wikipedia tastes better and is less filling than the Encyclopedia Galactica.')

In the 1980s, during what has been referred to as the cola wars, soft-drink manufacturer Pepsi ran a series of advertisements where people, caught on hidden camera, in a blind taste test, chose Pepsi over rival Coca-Cola.

## Chapter 12. INDEPENDENT DEMAND INVENTORY MANAGEMENT

a. 28-hour day
b. 1990 Clean Air Act
c. 33 Strategies of War
d. Comparative advertising

8. The _____ is an equation that equals the cost of goods sold divided by the average inventory. Average inventory equals beginning inventory plus ending inventory divided by 2.

The formula for _____:

>

The formula for average inventory:

>

A low turnover rate may point to overstocking, obsolescence, or deficiencies in the product line or marketing effort.

a. Inventory turnover
b. A4e
c. Asset turnover
d. A Stake in the Outcome

9. In economics, business, retail, and accounting, a _____ is the value of money that has been used up to produce something, and hence is not available for use anymore. In economics, a _____ is an alternative that is given up as a result of a decision. In business, the _____ may be one of acquisition, in which case the amount of money expended to acquire it is counted as _____.

a. Fixed costs
b. Cost overrun
c. Cost allocation
d. Cost

10. In a human resources context, _____ or labor _____ is the rate at which an employer gains and loses employees. Simple ways to describe it are 'how long employees tend to stay' or 'the rate of traffic through the revolving door.' _____ is measured for individual companies and for their industry as a whole. If an employer is said to have a high _____ relative to its competitors, it means that employees of that company have a shorter average tenure than those of other companies in the same industry.

## Chapter 12. INDEPENDENT DEMAND INVENTORY MANAGEMENT

  a. Ten year occupational employment projection
  b. Career portfolios
  c. Continuous
  d. Turnover

11. _____ are costs incurred on the purchase of land, buildings, construction and equipment to be used in the production of goods or the rendering of services. In other words, the total cost needed to bring a project to a commercially operable status. However, _____ are not limited to the initial construction of a factory or other business.

  a. Contingent employment
  b. Capital costs
  c. Reservation wage
  d. Fixed asset turnover

12. In business management, _____ is money spent to keep and maintain a stock of goods in storage.

The most obvious _____s include rent for the required space; equipment, materials, and labor to operate the space; insurance; security; interest on money invested in the inventory and space, and other direct expenses. Some stored goods become obsolete before they are sold, reducing their contribution to revenue while having no effect on their _____.

  a. Holding cost
  b. Private placement
  c. Choquet integral
  d. Market niche

13. In decision theory and estimation theory, the _____ of an estimator, $\hat{\theta}$, of an unknown parameter of the distribution, θ, is the expected value of the loss function

$$R(\theta, \hat{\theta}) = \mathbb{E}_\theta L(\theta, \hat{\theta}) = \int L(\theta, \hat{\theta})\, dP_\theta.$$

## Chapter 12. INDEPENDENT DEMAND INVENTORY MANAGEMENT

where $dP_\theta$ is a probability measure parametrized by θ.

- For a scalar parameter θ and a quadratic loss function,

$$L(\theta, \hat{\theta}) = (\theta - \hat{\theta})^2$$

the _____ function becomes the mean squared error of the estimate,

$$R(\theta, \hat{\theta}) = E_\theta (\theta - \hat{\theta})^2$$

- In density estimation, the unknown parameter is probability density itself. The loss function is typically chosen to be a norm in an appropriate function space. For example, for $L^2$ norm,

$$L(f, \hat{f}) = \|f - \hat{f}\|_2^2$$

the _____ function becomes the mean integrated squared error

$$R(f, \hat{f}) = E\|f - \hat{f}\|^2$$

a. Linear model
b. Risk
c. Financial modeling
d. Risk aversion


14. In probability theory, a probability distribution is called _____ if its cumulative distribution function is _____. This is equivalent to saying that for random variables X with the distribution in question, Pr[X = a] = 0 for all real numbers a, i.e.: the probability that X attains the value a is zero, for any number a. If the distribution of X is _____ then X is called a _____ random variable.
   a. Continuous
   b. Connectionist expert systems
   c. Decision tree pruning
   d. Pay Band


15. _____ is the level of inventory that minimizes the total inventory holding costs and ordering costs. The framework used to determine this order quantity is also known as Wilson _____ Model. The model was developed by F. W. Harris in 1913.

## Chapter 12. INDEPENDENT DEMAND INVENTORY MANAGEMENT

a. Anti-leadership
b. Economic order quantity
c. Effective executive
d. Event management

16. _____ of the learning curve effect and the closely related experience curve effect express the relationship between equations for experience and efficiency or between efficiency gains and investment in the effort. The experience of 'learning curves' was first observed by the 19th Century German psychologist Hermann Ebbinghaus according to the difficulty of memorizing varying numbers of verbal stimuli, and subsequent learning about the complex processes of learning are discussed in the

.

The rule used for representing the learning curve effect states that the more times a task has been performed, the less time will be required on each subsequent iteration.

a. Distribution
b. Spatial Decision Support Systems
c. Point biserial correlation coefficient
d. Models

17. A _____ is the period of time between the initiation of any process of production and the completion of that process. Thus the _____ for ordering a new car from a manufacturer may be anywhere from 2 weeks to 6 months. In industry, _____ reduction is an important part of lean manufacturing.

a. 1990 Clean Air Act
b. 33 Strategies of War
c. 28-hour day
d. Lead time

18. A _____ is typically described as a deliberate plan of action to guide decisions and achieve rational outcome(s.) However, the term may also be used to denote what is actually done, even though it is unplanned.

The term may apply to government, private sector organizations and groups, and individuals.

a. 28-hour day
b. Policy
c. 33 Strategies of War
d. 1990 Clean Air Act

## Chapter 12. INDEPENDENT DEMAND INVENTORY MANAGEMENT

19. _____ model is an extension of the Economic Order Quantity model. The _____ model was developed by E.W. Taft in 1918. The difference being that the _____ model assumes orders are received incrementally during the production process.
   a. A4e
   b. A Stake in the Outcome
   c. Economies of scope
   d. Economic production quantity

20. _____ measures the performance of a system. Certain goals are defined and the _____ gives the percentage to which they should be achieved.

Examples

- Percentage of calls answered in a call center.
- Percentage of customers waiting less than a given fixed time.
- Percentage of customers that do not experience a stock out.

_____ is used in supply chain management and in inventory management to measure the performance of inventory systems.

Under stochastic conditions it is unavoidable that in some periods the inventory on hand is not sufficient to deliver the complete demand and, as a consequence, that part of the demand is filled only after an inventory-related waiting time.

   a. 28-hour day
   b. 33 Strategies of War
   c. 1990 Clean Air Act
   d. Service level

21. In the fields of science, engineering, industry and statistics, _____ is the degree of closeness of a measured or calculated quantity to its actual (true) value. _____ is closely related to precision, also called reproducibility or repeatability, the degree to which further measurements or calculations show the same or similar results. _____ indicates proximity to the true value, precision to the repeatability or reproducibility of the measurement

The results of calculations or a measurement can be accurate but not precise, precise but not accurate, neither, or both.

a. A Stake in the Outcome
b. Accuracy
c. AAAI
d. A4e

22. _____ is a family of business models in which the buyer of a product provides certain information to a supplier of that product and the supplier takes full responsibility for maintaining an agreed inventory of the material, usually at the buyer's consumption location (usually a store.) A third party logistics provider can also be involved to make sure that the buyer has the required level of inventory by adjusting the demand and supply gaps.

As a symbiotic relationship, _____ makes it less likely that a business will unintentionally become out of stock of a good and reduces inventory in the supply chain.

a. Vendor Managed Inventory
b. Supply Chain Risk Management
c. Delayed differentiation
d. Supply-Chain Operations Reference

23. _____ is an area of business concerned with the production of goods and services, and involves the responsibility of ensuring that business operations are efficient in terms of using as little resource as needed, and effective in terms of meeting customer requirements. It is concerned with managing the process that converts inputs (in the forms of materials, labour and energy) into outputs (in the form of goods and services.)

Operations traditionally refers to the production of goods and services separately, although the distinction between these two main types of operations is increasingly difficult to make as manufacturers tend to merge product and service offerings.

a. A4e
b. Operations management
c. AAAI
d. A Stake in the Outcome

24. _____ is an integrated communications-based process through which individuals and communities discover that existing and newly-identified needs and wants may be satisfied by the products and services of others.

_____ is defined by the American _____ Association as the activity, set of institutions, and processes for creating, communicating, delivering, and exchanging offerings that have value for customers, clients, partners, and society at large. The term developed from the original meaning which referred literally to going to market, as in shopping, or going to a market to buy or sell goods or services.

a. Customer relationship management
b. Marketing
c. Market development
d. Disruptive technology



25. A _____ is the system of organizations, people, technology, activities, information and resources involved in moving a product or service from supplier to customer. _____ activities transform natural resources, raw materials and components into a finished product that is delivered to the end customer. In sophisticated _____ systems, used products may re-enter the _____ at any point where residual value is recyclable.

a. Wholesalers
b. Drop shipping
c. Packaging
d. Supply chain



26. _____ is the management of a network of interconnected businesses involved in the ultimate provision of product and service packages required by end customers (Harland, 1996.) _____ spans all movement and storage of raw materials, work-in-process inventory, and finished goods from point of origin to point of consumption (supply chain.)

The definition an American professional association put forward is that _____ encompasses the planning and management of all activities involved in sourcing, procurement, conversion, and logistics management activities.

a. Freight forwarder
b. Drop shipping
c. Supply chain management
d. Packaging



27. _____ is an operational activity which does an aggregate plan for the production process, in advance of 2 to 18 months, to give an idea to management as to what quantity of materials and other resources are to be procured and when, so that the total cost of operations of the organization is kept to the minimum over that period.

The quantity of outsourcing, subcontracting of items, overtime of labor, numbers to be hired and fired in each period and the amount of inventory to be held in stock and to be backlogged for each period are decided. All of these activities are done within the framework of the company ethics, policies, and long term commitment to the society, community and the country of operation.

a. Earned value management
b. A Stake in the Outcome
c. Aggregate planning
d. Earned Schedule

## Chapter 13. AGGREGATE PLANNING

1. _____ is an operational activity which does an aggregate plan for the production process, in advance of 2 to 18 months, to give an idea to management as to what quantity of materials and other resources are to be procured and when, so that the total cost of operations of the organization is kept to the minimum over that period.

The quantity of outsourcing, subcontracting of items, overtime of labor, numbers to be hired and fired in each period and the amount of inventory to be held in stock and to be backlogged for each period are decided. All of these activities are done within the framework of the company ethics, policies, and long term commitment to the society, community and the country of operation.

   a. Aggregate planning
   b. Earned Schedule
   c. A Stake in the Outcome
   d. Earned value management


2. _____ is an integrated communications-based process through which individuals and communities discover that existing and newly-identified needs and wants may be satisfied by the products and services of others.

_____ is defined by the American _____ Association as the activity, set of institutions, and processes for creating, communicating, delivering, and exchanging offerings that have value for customers, clients, partners, and society at large. The term developed from the original meaning which referred literally to going to market, as in shopping, or going to a market to buy or sell goods or services.

   a. Market development
   b. Marketing
   c. Disruptive technology
   d. Customer relationship management


3. A _____ is a formal statement of a set of business goals, the reasons why they are believed attainable, and the plan for reaching those goals. It may also contain background information about the organization or team attempting to reach those goals.

The business goals may be defined for for-profit or for non-profit organizations.

   a. Time management
   b. Crisis management
   c. Distributed management
   d. Business plan


4. A _____ is a written document that details the necessary actions to achieve one or more marketing objectives. It can be for a product or service, a brand, or a product line. _____s cover between one and five years.

## Chapter 13. AGGREGATE PLANNING

a. Marketing plan
b. Disruptive technology
c. Market development
d. Marketing strategy

5. A _____ is a plan for production, staffing, inventory, etc. It is usually linked to manufacturing where the plan indicates when and how much of each product will be demanded. This plan quantifies significant processes, parts, and other resources in order to optimize production, to identify bottlenecks, and to anticipate needs and completed goods.
   a. Value engineering
   b. Piecework
   c. Remanufacturing
   d. Master production schedule

6. _____ is an inventory strategy that strives to improve the return on investment of a business by reducing in-process inventory and its associated carrying costs. To meet _____ objectives, the process relies on signals between different points in the process. This means the process is often driven by a series of signals, or Kanban, which tell production when to make the next part. Kanban are usually 'tickets' but can be simple visual signals, such as the presence or absence of a part on a shelf. Implemented correctly, _____ can dramatically improve a manufacturing organization's return on investment, quality, and efficiency.
   a. 28-hour day
   b. 33 Strategies of War
   c. Just-in-time
   d. 1990 Clean Air Act

7. _____ are goods that have completed the manufacturing process but have not yet been sold or distributed to the end user.

Manufacturing has three classes of inventory:

1. Raw material
2. Work in process
3. _____

A good purchased as a 'raw material' goes into the manufacture of a product. A good only partially completed during the manufacturing process is called 'work in process'. When the good is completed as to manufacturing but not yet sold or distributed to the end-user is called a 'finished good'.

a. 1990 Clean Air Act
b. 28-hour day
c. Reorder point
d. Finished goods


8. In finance, an _____ is a contract between a buyer and a seller that gives the buyer the right--but not the obligation-- to buy or to sell a particular asset (the underlying asset) at a later day at an agreed price. In return for granting the _____, the seller collects a payment (the premium) from the buyer. A call _____ gives the buyer the right to buy the underlying asset; a put _____ gives the buyer of the _____ the right to sell the underlying asset.

a. A Stake in the Outcome
b. A4e
c. AAAI
d. Option


9. _____ in its literal sense is the process of transformation of local or regional phenomena into global ones. It can be described as a process by which the people of the world are unified into a single society and function together.

This process is a combination of economic, technological, sociocultural and political forces.

a. Cost Management
b. Globalization
c. Histogram
d. Collaborative Planning, Forecasting and Replenishment


10. _____ is the amount of time someone works beyond normal working hours. Normal hours may be determined in several ways:

- by custom (what is considered healthy or reasonable by society),
- by practices of a given trade or profession,
- by legislation,
- by agreement between employers and workers or their representatives.

Most nations have _____ laws designed to dissuade or prevent employers from forcing their employees to work excessively long hours. These laws may take into account other considerations than the humanitarian, such as increasing the overall level of employment in the economy. One common approach to regulating _____ is to require employers to pay workers at a higher hourly rate for _____ work.

a. Organizational structure
b. Organizational effectiveness
c. Industrial relations
d. Overtime

11. In economics, _____ is the desire to own something and the ability to pay for it. The term _____ signifies the ability or the willingness to buy a particular commodity at a given point of time.
    a. 1990 Clean Air Act
    b. 33 Strategies of War
    c. 28-hour day
    d. Demand

12. _____ is the act by an employer of terminating employment. Though such a decision can be made by an employer for a variety of reasons, ranging from an economic downturn to performance-related problems on the part of the employee, being fired has a strong stigma in many cultures. To be fired, as opposed to quitting voluntarily (or being laid off), is often perceived as being the employee's fault, and is therefore considered to be disgraceful and a sign of failure.
    a. Severance package
    b. Firing
    c. Layoff
    d. Termination of employment

13. _____ occurs when a person is available to work and seeking work but currently without work. The prevalence of _____ is usually measured using the _____ rate, which is defined as the percentage of those in the labor force who are unemployed. The _____ rate is also used in economic studies and economic indexes such as the United States' Conference Board's Index of Leading Indicators as a measure of the state of the macroeconomics.
    a. Employment-to-population ratio
    b. Outplacement
    c. Unemployment Convention, 1919
    d. Unemployment

14. _____ is money received by an unemployed worker from the United States or a state. In the United States, this compensation is classified as a type of social welfare benefit. According to the Internal Revenue Code, these types of benefits are to be included in a taxpayer's gross income.

## Chapter 13. AGGREGATE PLANNING

a. Unemployment
b. Unemployment insurance
c. Unemployment compensation
d. Unemployment Provision Convention, 1934

15. _____ is an advertisement in which a particular product specifically mentions a competitor by name for the express purpose of showing why the competitor is inferior to the product naming it.

This should not be confused with parody advertisements, where a fictional product is being advertised for the purpose of poking fun at the particular advertisement, nor should it be confused with the use of a coined brand name for the purpose of comparing the product without actually naming an actual competitor. ('Wikipedia tastes better and is less filling than the Encyclopedia Galactica.')

In the 1980s, during what has been referred to as the cola wars, soft-drink manufacturer Pepsi ran a series of advertisements where people, caught on hidden camera, in a blind taste test, chose Pepsi over rival Coca-Cola.

a. Comparative advertising
b. 1990 Clean Air Act
c. 33 Strategies of War
d. 28-hour day

16. In economics, _____' is the art or science of controlling economic demand to avoid a recession. In natural resources management and environmental policy more generally, it refers to policies to control consumer demand for environmentally sensitive or harmful goods such as water and energy. Within manufacturing firms the term is used to describe the activities of demand forecasting, planning and order fulfillment.

a. 1990 Clean Air Act
b. 28-hour day
c. 33 Strategies of War
d. Demand management

17. _____ is a software based production planning and inventory control system used to manage manufacturing processes. Although it is not common nowadays, it is possible to conduct _____ by hand as well.

An _____ system is intended to simultaneously meet three objectives:

- Ensure materials and products are available for production and delivery to customers.
- Maintain the lowest possible level of inventory.
- Plan manufacturing activities, delivery schedules and purchasing activities.

Manufacturing organizations, whatever their products, face the same daily practical problem - that customers want products to be available in a shorter time than it takes to make them. This means that some level of planning is required.

- a. 28-hour day
- b. 33 Strategies of War
- c. Material requirements planning
- d. 1990 Clean Air Act

18. _____ is the process of determining the production capacity needed by an organization to meet changing demands for its products. In the context of _____, 'capacity' is the maximum amount of work that an organization is capable of completing in a given period of time.

A discrepancy between the capacity of an organization and the demands of its customers results in inefficiency, either in under-utilized resources or unfulfilled customers.

- a. Remanufacturing
- b. Productivity
- c. Scientific management
- d. Capacity planning

19. _____ is a business function that provides a response to customer order enquiries, based on resource availability. It generates available quantities of the requested product, and delivery due dates. Therefore, _____ supports order promising and fulfillment, aiming to manage demand and match it to production plans.
- a. A4e
- b. A Stake in the Outcome
- c. AAAI
- d. Available-to-promise

20. _____ is an area of business concerned with the production of goods and services, and involves the responsibility of ensuring that business operations are efficient in terms of using as little resource as needed, and effective in terms of meeting customer requirements. It is concerned with managing the process that converts inputs (in the forms of materials, labour and energy) into outputs (in the form of goods and services.)

Operations traditionally refers to the production of goods and services separately, although the distinction between these two main types of operations is increasingly difficult to make as manufacturers tend to merge product and service offerings.

## Chapter 13. AGGREGATE PLANNING

a. AAAI
b. A Stake in the Outcome
c. A4e
d. Operations management


21. A _____ is the system of organizations, people, technology, activities, information and resources involved in moving a product or service from supplier to customer. _____ activities transform natural resources, raw materials and components into a finished product that is delivered to the end customer. In sophisticated _____ systems, used products may re-enter the _____ at any point where residual value is recyclable.
   a. Packaging
   b. Wholesalers
   c. Drop shipping
   d. Supply chain


22. _____ is the management of a network of interconnected businesses involved in the ultimate provision of product and service packages required by end customers (Harland, 1996.) _____ spans all movement and storage of raw materials, work-in-process inventory, and finished goods from point of origin to point of consumption (supply chain.)

The definition an American professional association put forward is that _____ encompasses the planning and management of all activities involved in sourcing, procurement, conversion, and logistics management activities.

   a. Packaging
   b. Freight forwarder
   c. Drop shipping
   d. Supply chain management

## Chapter 14. RESOURCE PLANNING

1. _____ is a company-wide computer software system used to manage and coordinate all the resources, information, and functions of a business from shared data stores.

An _____ system has a service-oriented architecture with modular hardware and software units and 'services' that communicate on a local area network. The modular design allows a business to add or reconfigure modules (perhaps from different vendors) while preserving data integrity in one shared database that may be centralized or distributed.

   a. AAAI
   b. A4e
   c. A Stake in the Outcome
   d. Enterprise resource planning


2. In business and accounting, _____s are everything of value that is owned by a person or company. Any property or object of value that one possesses, usually considered as applicable to the payment of one's debts is considered an _____. Simplistically stated, _____s are things of value that can be readily converted into cash.
   a. A Stake in the Outcome
   b. AAAI
   c. Asset
   d. A4e


3. A _____ is the system of organizations, people, technology, activities, information and resources involved in moving a product or service from supplier to customer. _____ activities transform natural resources, raw materials and components into a finished product that is delivered to the end customer. In sophisticated _____ systems, used products may re-enter the _____ at any point where residual value is recyclable.
   a. Supply chain
   b. Packaging
   c. Wholesalers
   d. Drop shipping


4. _____ is the management of a network of interconnected businesses involved in the ultimate provision of product and service packages required by end customers (Harland, 1996.) _____ spans all movement and storage of raw materials, work-in-process inventory, and finished goods from point of origin to point of consumption (supply chain.)

The definition an American professional association put forward is that _____ encompasses the planning and management of all activities involved in sourcing, procurement, conversion, and logistics management activities.

a. Freight forwarder
b. Packaging
c. Supply chain management
d. Drop shipping


5. _____ is a business term which refers to a range of software tools or modules used in executing supply chain transactions, managing supplier relationships and controlling associated business processes.

While functionality in such systems can often be broad - it commonly includes:

1. Customer requirement processing
2. Purchase order processing
3. Inventory management
4. Goods receipt and Warehouse management
5. Supplier Management/Sourcing

A requirement of many _____ often includes forecasting. Such tools often attempt to balance the disparity between supply and demand by improving business processes and using algorithms and consumption analysis to better plan future needs. _____ also often includes integration technology that allows organizations to trade electronically with supply chain partners.

a. Demand chain
b. Supply-Chain Operations Reference
c. Vendor Managed Inventory
d. Supply chain management software


6. _____ is an advertisement in which a particular product specifically mentions a competitor by name for the express purpose of showing why the competitor is inferior to the product naming it.

This should not be confused with parody advertisements, where a fictional product is being advertised for the purpose of poking fun at the particular advertisement, nor should it be confused with the use of a coined brand name for the purpose of comparing the product without actually naming an actual competitor. ('Wikipedia tastes better and is less filling than the Encyclopedia Galactica.')

In the 1980s, during what has been referred to as the cola wars, soft-drink manufacturer Pepsi ran a series of advertisements where people, caught on hidden camera, in a blind taste test, chose Pepsi over rival Coca-Cola.

a. 33 Strategies of War
b. 1990 Clean Air Act
c. 28-hour day
d. Comparative advertising

7. _____, commonly known as e-commerce, consists of the buying and selling of products or services over electronic systems such as the Internet and other computer networks. The amount of trade conducted electronically has grown extraordinarily with widespread Internet usage. The use of commerce is conducted in this way, spurring and drawing on innovations in electronic funds transfer, supply chain management, Internet marketing, online transaction processing, electronic data interchange (EDI), inventory management systems, and automated data collection systems.
   a. Electronic Commerce
   b. A4e
   c. Online shopping
   d. A Stake in the Outcome

8. In economics, business, retail, and accounting, a _____ is the value of money that has been used up to produce something, and hence is not available for use anymore. In economics, a _____ is an alternative that is given up as a result of a decision. In business, the _____ may be one of acquisition, in which case the amount of money expended to acquire it is counted as _____.
   a. Cost allocation
   b. Cost overrun
   c. Fixed costs
   d. Cost

9. A _____ is a plan for production, staffing, inventory, etc. It is usually linked to manufacturing where the plan indicates when and how much of each product will be demanded. This plan quantifies significant processes, parts, and other resources in order to optimize production, to identify bottlenecks, and to anticipate needs and completed goods.
   a. Master production schedule
   b. Piecework
   c. Value engineering
   d. Remanufacturing

10. _____ is a software based production planning and inventory control system used to manage manufacturing processes. Although it is not common nowadays, it is possible to conduct _____ by hand as well.

## Chapter 14. RESOURCE PLANNING

An _____ system is intended to simultaneously meet three objectives:

- Ensure materials and products are available for production and delivery to customers.
- Maintain the lowest possible level of inventory.
- Plan manufacturing activities, delivery schedules and purchasing activities.

Manufacturing organizations, whatever their products, face the same daily practical problem - that customers want products to be available in a shorter time than it takes to make them. This means that some level of planning is required.

a. 33 Strategies of War
b. 28-hour day
c. 1990 Clean Air Act
d. Material requirements planning


11. _____ is a list of the raw materials, sub-assemblies, intermediate assemblies, sub-components, components, parts and the quantities of each needed to manufacture an end item (final product) .
a. Scientific management
b. Bill of materials
c. Methods-time measurement
d. Piece rate


12. In economics, _____ is the desire to own something and the ability to pay for it. The term _____ signifies the ability or the willingness to buy a particular commodity at a given point of time.
a. 33 Strategies of War
b. 28-hour day
c. Demand
d. 1990 Clean Air Act


13. A _____ is the period of time between the initiation of any process of production and the completion of that process. Thus the _____ for ordering a new car from a manufacturer may be anywhere from 2 weeks to 6 months. In industry, _____ reduction is an important part of lean manufacturing.
a. Lead time
b. 33 Strategies of War
c. 1990 Clean Air Act
d. 28-hour day

## Chapter 14. RESOURCE PLANNING

14. In the fields of science, engineering, industry and statistics, _____ is the degree of closeness of a measured or calculated quantity to its actual (true) value. _____ is closely related to precision, also called reproducibility or repeatability, the degree to which further measurements or calculations show the same or similar results. _____ indicates proximity to the true value, precision to the repeatability or reproducibility of the measurement

The results of calculations or a measurement can be accurate but not precise, precise but not accurate, neither, or both.

   a. A4e
   b. Accuracy
   c. A Stake in the Outcome
   d. AAAI

15. In terms of United States labor relations, an _____ is a place of employment at which one is not required to join or financially support a labor union as a condition of hiring or continued employment. _____s are required by law in right-to-work jurisdictions and employers such as the Federal government of the United States. In contrast, a closed shop is one in which all employees must be members of a union prior to being employed, and a union shop is one in which an employee must become a member in order to retain employment.
   a. Union shop
   b. Organizational development
   c. Open shop
   d. Organizational culture

16. _____ is an area of business concerned with the production of goods and services, and involves the responsibility of ensuring that business operations are efficient in terms of using as little resource as needed, and effective in terms of meeting customer requirements. It is concerned with managing the process that converts inputs (in the forms of materials, labour and energy) into outputs (in the form of goods and services.)

Operations traditionally refers to the production of goods and services separately, although the distinction between these two main types of operations is increasingly difficult to make as manufacturers tend to merge product and service offerings.

   a. AAAI
   b. A4e
   c. Operations management
   d. A Stake in the Outcome

17. _____ is an integrated communications-based process through which individuals and communities discover that existing and newly-identified needs and wants may be satisfied by the products and services of others.

## Chapter 14. RESOURCE PLANNING

_____ is defined by the American _____ Association as the activity, set of institutions, and processes for creating, communicating, delivering, and exchanging offerings that have value for customers, clients, partners, and society at large. The term developed from the original meaning which referred literally to going to market, as in shopping, or going to a market to buy or sell goods or services.

a. Market development
b. Customer relationship management
c. Disruptive technology
d. Marketing


18. _____ is an operational activity which does an aggregate plan for the production process, in advance of 2 to 18 months, to give an idea to management as to what quantity of materials and other resources are to be procured and when, so that the total cost of operations of the organization is kept to the minimum over that period.

The quantity of outsourcing, subcontracting of items, overtime of labor, numbers to be hired and fired in each period and the amount of inventory to be held in stock and to be backlogged for each period are decided. All of these activities are done within the framework of the company ethics, policies, and long term commitment to the society, community and the country of operation.

a. Earned value management
b. Earned Schedule
c. A Stake in the Outcome
d. Aggregate planning

## Chapter 15. SCHEDULING

1. A _____ is a type of bar chart that illustrates a project schedule. _____s illustrate the start and finish dates of the terminal elements and summary elements of a project. Terminal elements and summary elements comprise the work breakdown structure of the project.
   a. 33 Strategies of War
   b. 28-hour day
   c. 1990 Clean Air Act
   d. Gantt chart

2. A _____ is a depiction of a sequence of operations, declared as work of a person, a group of persons, an organization of staff, or one or more simple or complex mechanisms. _____ may be seen as any abstraction of real work, segregated in workshare, work split or other types of ordering. For control purposes, _____ may be a view on real work under a chosen aspect, thus serving as a virtual representation of actual work.
   a. Resource-based view
   b. Time management
   c. Management development
   d. Workflow

3. _____ is one of the managerial functions like planning, organizing, staffing and directing. It is an important function because it helps to check the errors and to take the corrective action so that deviation from standards are minimized and stated goals of the organization are achieved in desired manner. According to modern concepts, _____ is a foreseeing action whereas earlier concept of _____ was used only when errors were detected. _____ in management means setting standards, measuring actual performance and taking corrective action.
   a. Schedule of reinforcement
   b. Decision tree pruning
   c. Turnover
   d. Control

4. _____ is the process whereby an organization establishes the parameters within which programs, investments, and acquisitions are reaching the desired results. Performance Reference Model of the Federal Enterprise Architecture, 2005.

This process of measuring performance often requires the use of statistical evidence to determine progress toward specific defined organizational objectives.

There are many types of measurements.

a. CIFMS
b. Crisis management
c. Performance measurement
d. Workflow


5. _____ is an advertisement in which a particular product specifically mentions a competitor by name for the express purpose of showing why the competitor is inferior to the product naming it.

This should not be confused with parody advertisements, where a fictional product is being advertised for the purpose of poking fun at the particular advertisement, nor should it be confused with the use of a coined brand name for the purpose of comparing the product without actually naming an actual competitor. ('Wikipedia tastes better and is less filling than the Encyclopedia Galactica.')

In the 1980s, during what has been referred to as the cola wars, soft-drink manufacturer Pepsi ran a series of advertisements where people, caught on hidden camera, in a blind taste test, chose Pepsi over rival Coca-Cola.

a. Comparative advertising
b. 1990 Clean Air Act
c. 33 Strategies of War
d. 28-hour day


6. _____ is an overall management philosophy introduced by Dr. Eliyahu M. Goldratt in his 1984 book titled The Goal, that is geared to help organizations continually achieve their goal. The title comes from the contention that any manageable system is limited in achieving more of its goal by a very small number of constraints, and that there is always at least one constraint. The _____ process seeks to identify the constraint and restructure the rest of the organization around it, through the use of the Five Focusing Steps.
a. Takt time
b. Six Sigma
c. Production line
d. Theory of constraints


7. A _____ is typically described as a deliberate plan of action to guide decisions and achieve rational outcome(s.) However, the term may also be used to denote what is actually done, even though it is unplanned.

The term may apply to government, private sector organizations and groups, and individuals.

a. 33 Strategies of War
b. Policy
c. 1990 Clean Air Act
d. 28-hour day

8. In economics, _____ is the desire to own something and the ability to pay for it. The term _____ signifies the ability or the willingness to buy a particular commodity at a given point of time.
   a. 28-hour day
   b. 1990 Clean Air Act
   c. 33 Strategies of War
   d. Demand

9. The _____ is the labour pool in employment. It is generally used to describe those working for a single company or industry, but can also apply to a geographic region like a city, country, state, etc. The term generally excludes the employers or management, and implies those involved in manual labour.
   a. Pink-collar worker
   b. Division of labour
   c. Workforce
   d. Work-life balance

10. _____ is an area of business concerned with the production of goods and services, and involves the responsibility of ensuring that business operations are efficient in terms of using as little resource as needed, and effective in terms of meeting customer requirements. It is concerned with managing the process that converts inputs (in the forms of materials, labour and energy) into outputs (in the form of goods and services.)

Operations traditionally refers to the production of goods and services separately, although the distinction between these two main types of operations is increasingly difficult to make as manufacturers tend to merge product and service offerings.

   a. AAAI
   b. Operations management
   c. A Stake in the Outcome
   d. A4e

11. _____ is an integrated communications-based process through which individuals and communities discover that existing and newly-identified needs and wants may be satisfied by the products and services of others.

## Chapter 15. SCHEDULING

_____ is defined by the American _____ Association as the activity, set of institutions, and processes for creating, communicating, delivering, and exchanging offerings that have value for customers, clients, partners, and society at large. The term developed from the original meaning which referred literally to going to market, as in shopping, or going to a market to buy or sell goods or services.

a. Customer relationship management
b. Market development
c. Disruptive technology
d. Marketing


12. _____ is an operational activity which does an aggregate plan for the production process, in advance of 2 to 18 months, to give an idea to management as to what quantity of materials and other resources are to be procured and when, so that the total cost of operations of the organization is kept to the minimum over that period.

The quantity of outsourcing, subcontracting of items, overtime of labor, numbers to be hired and fired in each period and the amount of inventory to be held in stock and to be backlogged for each period are decided. All of these activities are done within the framework of the company ethics, policies, and long term commitment to the society, community and the country of operation.

a. A Stake in the Outcome
b. Earned value management
c. Earned Schedule
d. Aggregate planning


13. A _____ is the system of organizations, people, technology, activities, information and resources involved in moving a product or service from supplier to customer. _____ activities transform natural resources, raw materials and components into a finished product that is delivered to the end customer. In sophisticated _____ systems, used products may re-enter the _____ at any point where residual value is recyclable.

a. Supply chain
b. Packaging
c. Wholesalers
d. Drop shipping


14. _____ is the management of a network of interconnected businesses involved in the ultimate provision of product and service packages required by end customers (Harland, 1996.) _____ spans all movement and storage of raw materials, work-in-process inventory, and finished goods from point of origin to point of consumption (supply chain.)

The definition an American professional association put forward is that _____ encompasses the planning and management of all activities involved in sourcing, procurement, conversion, and logistics management activities.

a. Drop shipping
b. Freight forwarder
c. Packaging
d. Supply chain management

## Chapter 16. PROJECT MANAGEMENT

1. _____ refers to the movement of cash into or out of a business or financial product. It is usually measured during a specified, finite period of time. Measurement of _____ can be used

   - to determine a project's rate of return or value. The time of _____s into and out of projects are used as inputs in financial models such as internal rate of return, and net present value.
   - to determine problems with a business's liquidity. Being profitable does not necessarily mean being liquid. A company can fail because of a shortage of cash, even while profitable.
   - as an alternate measure of a business's profits when it is believed that accrual accounting concepts do not represent economic realities. For example, a company may be notionally profitable but generating little operational cash (as may be the case for a company that barters its products rather than selling for cash.) In such a case, the company may be deriving additional operating cash by issuing shares evaluating default risk, re-investment requirements, etc.

   _____ is a generic term used differently depending on the context. It may be defined by users for their own purposes.

   a. Gross profit
   b. Sweat equity
   c. Gross profit margin
   d. Cash flow

2. _____ is the discipline of planning, organizing and managing resources to bring about the successful completion of specific project goals and objectives. It is often closely related to and sometimes conflated with Program management.

   A project is a finite endeavor--having specific start and completion dates--undertaken to meet particular goals and objectives, usually to bring about beneficial change or added value.

   a. Precedence diagram
   b. Project engineer
   c. Work package
   d. Project management

3. _____ is a way of expressing knowledge or belief that an event will occur or has occurred. In mathematics the concept has been given an exact meaning in _____ theory, that is used extensively in such areas of study as mathematics, statistics, finance, gambling, science, and philosophy to draw conclusions about the likelihood of potential events and the underlying mechanics of complex systems.

   The word _____ does not have a consistent direct definition.

## Chapter 16. PROJECT MANAGEMENT

a. Time series analysis
b. Statistics
c. Standard deviation
d. Probability

4. The Program (or Project) Evaluation and Review Technique, commonly abbreviated _____, is a model for project management designed to analyze and represent the tasks involved in completing a given project.

_____ is a method to analyze the involved tasks in completing a given project, specially the time needed to complete each task, and identifying the minimum time needed to complete the total project.

_____ was developed primarily to simplify the planning and scheduling of large and complex projects.

a. 33 Strategies of War
b. 1990 Clean Air Act
c. 28-hour day
d. PERT

5. The _____, is a mathematically based algorithm for scheduling a set of project activities. It is an important tool for effective project management.

It was developed in the 1950s by the Dupont Corporation at about the same time that General Dynamics and the US Navy were developing the Program Evaluation and Review Technique (PERT) Today, it is commonly used with all forms of projects, including construction, software development, research projects, product development, engineering, and plant maintenance, among others.

a. 33 Strategies of War
b. 28-hour day
c. 1990 Clean Air Act
d. Critical path method

6. _____ is one of the four elements of marketing mix. An organization or set of organizations (go-betweens) involved in the process of making a product or service available for use or consumption by a consumer or business user.

The other three parts of the marketing mix are product, pricing, and promotion.

a. Matching theory
b. Missing completely at random
c. Job creation programs
d. Distribution


7. In probability theory and statistics, a _____ identifies either the probability of each value of an unidentified random variable (when the variable is discrete), or the probability of the value falling within a particular interval (when the variable is continuous.) The _____ describes the range of possible values that a random variable can attain and the probability that the value of the random variable is within any (measurable) subset of that range. The Normal distribution, often called the 'bell curve'

When the random variable takes values in the set of real numbers, the _____ is completely described by the cumulative distribution function, whose value at each real x is the probability that the random variable is smaller than or equal to x.

a. Median
b. Frequency distribution
c. Statistically significant
d. Probability distribution


8. _____ is a method of planning and managing projects that puts the main emphasis on the resources required to execute project tasks. It was developed by Eliyahu M. Goldratt. This is in contrast to the more traditional Critical Path and PERT methods, which emphasize task order and rigid scheduling. A Critical Chain project network will tend to keep the resources levelly loaded, but will require them to be flexible in their start times and to quickly switch between tasks and task chains to keep the whole project on schedule.
a. Project engineer
b. Critical Chain Project Management
c. Project management office
d. Precedence diagram


9. A _____ is a type of bar chart that illustrates a project schedule. _____s illustrate the start and finish dates of the terminal elements and summary elements of a project. Terminal elements and summary elements comprise the work breakdown structure of the project.
a. 33 Strategies of War
b. 28-hour day
c. 1990 Clean Air Act
d. Gantt chart

## Chapter 16. PROJECT MANAGEMENT

10. _____ is an integrated communications-based process through which individuals and communities discover that existing and newly-identified needs and wants may be satisfied by the products and services of others.

_____ is defined by the American _____ Association as the activity, set of institutions, and processes for creating, communicating, delivering, and exchanging offerings that have value for customers, clients, partners, and society at large. The term developed from the original meaning which referred literally to going to market, as in shopping, or going to a market to buy or sell goods or services.

a. Customer relationship management
b. Marketing
c. Disruptive technology
d. Market development

11. _____ is an area of business concerned with the production of goods and services, and involves the responsibility of ensuring that business operations are efficient in terms of using as little resource as needed, and effective in terms of meeting customer requirements. It is concerned with managing the process that converts inputs (in the forms of materials, labour and energy) into outputs (in the form of goods and services.)

Operations traditionally refers to the production of goods and services separately, although the distinction between these two main types of operations is increasingly difficult to make as manufacturers tend to merge product and service offerings.

a. A Stake in the Outcome
b. AAAI
c. Operations management
d. A4e

12. _____ is an operational activity which does an aggregate plan for the production process, in advance of 2 to 18 months, to give an idea to management as to what quantity of materials and other resources are to be procured and when, so that the total cost of operations of the organization is kept to the minimum over that period.

The quantity of outsourcing, subcontracting of items, overtime of labor, numbers to be hired and fired in each period and the amount of inventory to be held in stock and to be backlogged for each period are decided. All of these activities are done within the framework of the company ethics, policies, and long term commitment to the society, community and the country of operation.

a. A Stake in the Outcome
b. Earned value management
c. Aggregate planning
d. Earned Schedule

13. A _____ is the system of organizations, people, technology, activities, information and resources involved in moving a product or service from supplier to customer. _____ activities transform natural resources, raw materials and components into a finished product that is delivered to the end customer. In sophisticated _____ systems, used products may re-enter the _____ at any point where residual value is recyclable.
   a. Packaging
   b. Wholesalers
   c. Supply chain
   d. Drop shipping

14. _____ is the management of a network of interconnected businesses involved in the ultimate provision of product and service packages required by end customers (Harland, 1996.) _____ spans all movement and storage of raw materials, work-in-process inventory, and finished goods from point of origin to point of consumption (supply chain.)

The definition an American professional association put forward is that _____ encompasses the planning and management of all activities involved in sourcing, procurement, conversion, and logistics management activities.

   a. Supply chain management
   b. Packaging
   c. Freight forwarder
   d. Drop shipping

## Chapter 1
| | | | | | | | | | |
|---|---|---|---|---|---|---|---|---|---|
| 1. d | 2. d | 3. c | 4. d | 5. b | 6. d | 7. d | 8. d | 9. d | 10. a |
| 11. c | 12. a | 13. d | 14. b | 15. d | 16. d | 17. a | 18. d | 19. a | 20. b |
| 21. d | 22. a | 23. c | 24. b | 25. c | 26. a | 27. c | 28. d | 29. a | 30. d |
| 31. d | 32. b | 33. a | 34. c | 35. a | 36. d | 37. d | 38. d | 39. d | 40. a |
| 41. a | 42. c | | | | | | | | |

## Chapter 2
| | | | | | | | | | |
|---|---|---|---|---|---|---|---|---|---|
| 1. d | 2. b | 3. d | 4. b | 5. a | 6. c | 7. c | 8. c | 9. d | 10. d |
| 11. a | 12. a | 13. c | 14. d | 15. c | 16. d | 17. d | 18. d | | |

## Chapter 3
| | | | | | | | | | |
|---|---|---|---|---|---|---|---|---|---|
| 1. d | 2. b | 3. d | 4. d | 5. d | 6. a | 7. a | 8. a | 9. d | 10. b |
| 11. c | 12. d | 13. c | 14. d | 15. d | 16. c | 17. b | 18. b | 19. a | 20. d |
| 21. d | 22. a | 23. c | 24. a | 25. c | 26. d | 27. d | 28. c | 29. d | 30. c |
| 31. d | 32. c | 33. d | 34. d | 35. a | 36. a | | | | |

## Chapter 4
| | | | | | | | | | |
|---|---|---|---|---|---|---|---|---|---|
| 1. b | 2. d | 3. c | 4. d | 5. d | 6. b | 7. a | 8. c | 9. c | 10. d |
| 11. b | 12. a | 13. b | 14. d | 15. d | 16. d | 17. a | 18. a | 19. d | 20. d |
| 21. b | 22. d | 23. c | 24. a | 25. d | 26. b | 27. c | 28. d | 29. a | 30. b |
| 31. a | 32. d | 33. d | 34. d | 35. d | 36. d | 37. a | | | |

## Chapter 5
| | | | | | | | | | |
|---|---|---|---|---|---|---|---|---|---|
| 1. d | 2. c | 3. c | 4. c | 5. c | 6. d | 7. d | 8. a | 9. a | 10. b |
| 11. d | 12. d | 13. d | 14. d | 15. d | 16. a | 17. d | 18. d | 19. c | 20. d |
| 21. a | 22. b | 23. d | 24. d | 25. b | 26. d | 27. d | 28. d | 29. c | |

## Chapter 6
| | | | | | | | | | |
|---|---|---|---|---|---|---|---|---|---|
| 1. b | 2. d | 3. d | 4. b | 5. c | 6. c | 7. a | 8. a | 9. d | 10. c |
| 11. d | 12. d | 13. d | 14. d | 15. b | 16. d | 17. b | 18. d | 19. d | 20. d |
| 21. d | 22. d | 23. d | 24. d | | | | | | |

## Chapter 7
| | | | | | | | | | |
|---|---|---|---|---|---|---|---|---|---|
| 1. d | 2. d | 3. d | 4. a | 5. c | 6. b | 7. a | 8. b | 9. c | 10. d |
| 11. a | 12. a | 13. c | 14. c | 15. d | 16. d | 17. b | 18. d | 19. d | 20. c |
| 21. b | 22. d | 23. d | 24. c | | | | | | |

## Chapter 8
| | | | | | | | | | |
|---|---|---|---|---|---|---|---|---|---|
| 1. b | 2. d | 3. d | 4. b | 5. b | 6. b | 7. d | 8. a | 9. d | 10. d |
| 11. a | 12. d | 13. a | 14. d | 15. a | 16. d | 17. d | 18. a | 19. d | 20. d |
| 21. b | 22. d | 23. c | 24. b | | | | | | |

# ANSWER KEY

**Chapter 9**
| | | | | | | | | | |
|---|---|---|---|---|---|---|---|---|---|
| 1. d | 2. b | 3. b | 4. d | 5. b | 6. d | 7. d | 8. d | 9. d | 10. d |
| 11. b | 12. d | 13. a | 14. a | 15. c | 16. d | 17. d | 18. d | 19. a | 20. a |
| 21. d | 22. d | 23. d | | | | | | | |

**Chapter 10**
| | | | | | | | |
|---|---|---|---|---|---|---|---|
| 1. b | 2. a | 3. a | 4. d | 5. b | 6. c | 7. c | 8. d |

**Chapter 11**
| | | | | | | | | | |
|---|---|---|---|---|---|---|---|---|---|
| 1. a | 2. b | 3. b | 4. d | 5. d | 6. d | 7. b | 8. a | 9. d | 10. d |
| 11. d | 12. c | 13. b | 14. a | 15. b | 16. d | 17. a | 18. b | 19. d | 20. c |
| 21. a | 22. d | 23. d | 24. b | 25. c | 26. d | 27. b | 28. d | | |

**Chapter 12**
| | | | | | | | | | |
|---|---|---|---|---|---|---|---|---|---|
| 1. c | 2. d | 3. a | 4. b | 5. a | 6. c | 7. d | 8. a | 9. d | 10. d |
| 11. b | 12. a | 13. b | 14. a | 15. b | 16. d | 17. d | 18. b | 19. d | 20. d |
| 21. b | 22. a | 23. b | 24. b | 25. d | 26. c | 27. c | | | |

**Chapter 13**
| | | | | | | | | | |
|---|---|---|---|---|---|---|---|---|---|
| 1. a | 2. b | 3. d | 4. a | 5. d | 6. c | 7. d | 8. d | 9. b | 10. d |
| 11. d | 12. b | 13. d | 14. c | 15. a | 16. d | 17. c | 18. d | 19. d | 20. d |
| 21. d | 22. d | | | | | | | | |

**Chapter 14**
| | | | | | | | | | |
|---|---|---|---|---|---|---|---|---|---|
| 1. d | 2. c | 3. a | 4. c | 5. d | 6. d | 7. a | 8. d | 9. a | 10. d |
| 11. b | 12. c | 13. a | 14. b | 15. c | 16. c | 17. d | 18. d | | |

**Chapter 15**
| | | | | | | | | | |
|---|---|---|---|---|---|---|---|---|---|
| 1. d | 2. d | 3. d | 4. c | 5. a | 6. d | 7. b | 8. d | 9. c | 10. b |
| 11. d | 12. d | 13. a | 14. d | | | | | | |

**Chapter 16**
| | | | | | | | | | |
|---|---|---|---|---|---|---|---|---|---|
| 1. d | 2. d | 3. d | 4. d | 5. d | 6. d | 7. d | 8. b | 9. d | 10. b |
| 11. c | 12. c | 13. c | 14. a | | | | | | |

www.ingramcontent.com/pod-product-compliance
Lightning Source LLC
Chambersburg PA
CBHW082044230426
43670CB00016B/2771